Lab Manual for Linux+
Guide to Linux Certification

Third Edition

Lab Manual for Linux+ Guide to Linux Certification

Third Edition

Greg Tomsho

COURSE TECHNOLOGY
CENGAGE Learning·

Australia • Brazil • Japan • Korea • Mexico • Singapore • Spain • United Kingdom • United States

COURSE TECHNOLOGY
CENGAGE Learning·

Lab Manual for Linux+
Guide to Linux Certification,
Third Edition
Greg Tomsho

Vice President, Careers and Computing:
Dave Garza

Editor-in-Chief: Marie Lee

Acquisitions Editor: Nick Lombardi

Director, Development-Career and
Computing: Marah Bellegarde

Product Manager: Natalie Pashoukos

Development Editor: Lisa M. Lord

Editorial Assistant: Sarah Pickering

Senior Brand Manager: Kristin McNairy

Market Development Manager: Mark Linton

Senior Production Director: Wendy Troeger

Production Manager: Andrew Crouth

Content Project Manager: Brooke Baker

Art Director: GEX, Inc.

Media Editor: William Overocker

Cover image: www.Shutterstock.com

Library of Congress Control Number: 2010941575
ISBN 13: 978-1-111-54155-2
ISBN 10: 1-111-54155-8

Course Technology
20 Channel Center Street
Boston, MA 02210
USA

Cengage Learning is a leading provider of customized learning solutions with office locations around the globe, including Singapore, the United Kingdom, Australia, Mexico, Brazil, and Japan. Locate your local office at **international.cengage.com/region**.

Cengage Learning products are represented in Canada by Nelson Education, Ltd.

To learn more about Course Technology, visit
www.cengage.com/coursetechnology

Purchase any of our products at your local college store or at our preferred online store: **www.cengagebrain.com**.

Notice to the Reader
Publisher does not warrant or guarantee any of the products described herein or perform any independent analysis in connection with any of the product information contained herein. Publisher does not assume, and expressly disclaims, any obligation to obtain and include information other than that provided to it by the manufacturer. The reader is expressly warned to consider and adopt all safety precautions that might be indicated by the activities described herein and to avoid all potential hazards. By following the instructions contained herein, the reader willingly assumes all risks in connection with such instructions. The publisher makes no representations or warranties of any kind, including but not limited to, the warranties of fitness for particular purpose or merchantability, nor are any such representations implied with respect to the material set forth herein, and the publisher takes no responsibility with respect to such material. The publisher shall not be liable for any special, consequential, or exemplary damages resulting, in whole or part, from the readers' use of, or reliance upon, this material

Some of the product names and company names used in this book have been used for identification purposes only and may be trademarks or registered trademarks of their respective manufacturers and sellers.

Microsoft and the Office logo are either registered trademarks or trademarks of Microsoft Corporation in the United States and/or other countries. Course Technology, a part of Cengage Learning, is an independent entity from the Microsoft Corporation and not affiliated with Microsoft in any manner.

Any fictional data related to persons or companies or URLs used throughout this book is intended for instructional purposes only. At the time this book was printed, any such data was fictional and not belonging to any real persons or companies.

Course Technology, the Course Technology logo, and the Shelly Cashman Series® are registered trademarks used under license.

The labs in this manual use Linux Fedora 13, an open-source operating system that falls under the General Public License (GPL) for free open-source software. Fedora 13 is developed and maintained by the Fedora Project (*http://fedoraproject.org*), a worldwide community of people who build free software. Fedora is sponsored by Red Hat (*http://redhat.com*).

Course Technology, a part of Cengage Learning, reserves the right to revise this publication and make changes from time to time in its content without notice.

The programs in this book are for instructional purposes only. They have been tested with care, but are not guaranteed for any particular intent beyond educational purposes. The author and the publisher do not offer any warranties or representations, nor do they accept any liabilities with respect to the programs.

Printed in the United States of America
1 2 3 4 5 6 7 17 16 15 14 13

Table of Contents

Introduction

Hands-on learning is the best way to master the skills needed for CompTIA's Linux+ exam and a Linux-related career. This book contains hands-on labs that apply fundamental Linux concepts as they're used in the real world. In addition, each chapter offers review questions to reinforce your mastery of the topics. The organization of this book follows the same organization as Course Technology's *Linux+ Guide to Linux Certification*, and using the two together gives you an effective learning experience. This book is suitable for use in a beginning Linux administration course. As a prerequisite, students should have a fundamental understanding of general operating system concepts and at least one course in operating systems and introductory networking. This book is best used when accompanied by the Course Technology book *Linux+ Guide to Linux Certification* or another Linux+ textbook.

Features

To ensure a successful experience for instructors and students alike, this book includes the following features:

- **Linux+ certification objectives**—Each chapter lists the relevant objectives from the CompTIA Linux+ exam.
- **Lab objectives**—Every lab has a brief description and list of learning objectives.
- **Materials required**—Each lab includes information on access privileges, hardware, software, and other materials you need to perform the lab.
- **Completion times**—Every lab has an estimated completion time so that you can plan your activities more accurately.
- **Activity sections**—Labs are presented in manageable sections; additional background information is given when needed.
- **Step-by-step instructions**—Logical step-by-step instructions guide you through the hands-on activities in each lab.
- **Review questions**—Questions help reinforce concepts covered in the lab.

Minimum Hardware Requirements

These minimum hardware requirements might not be enough for running Fedora 13 in all situations, but they should be satisfactory for running the labs in this manual:

- 400 MHz Pentium Pro CPU or better
- 10 GB hard disk space
- 512 MB memory (RAM)
- CD/DVD-ROM drive
- One PCI Ethernet network interface card
- Internet connection

Software and Setup Requirements

- Fedora 13
- Any Web browser
- Two blank DVDs

Acknowledgments

Thanks to Lisa Lord, development editor, who artfully takes a rough manuscript, smoothes out the edges, and makes it readable. Thanks also go to Natalie Pashoukos, Course Technology/Cengage Learning Product Manager, for giving me an opportunity to update this lab manual; Brooke Baker, Content Project Manager, for coordinating this book's production; and Serge Palladino for testing the labs and making corrections and suggestions as needed.

INTRODUCTION TO LINUX

Labs included in this chapter

- Lab 1.1 Becoming Familiar with the Squid Proxy Server
- Lab 1.2 Exploring Different Linux Distributions
- Lab 1.3 Exploring Open-Source Software
- Lab 1.4 Seeing How Linux and Windows Can Be Integrated
- Lab 1.5 Investigating Linux Security

CompTIA Linux+ Exam Objectives

Objective		Lab
N/A	These labs don't address Linux+ objectives directly, but they give you background information to help you master the objectives and understand the Linux operating system.	1.1–1.5

 Some labs in this book explore information on the World Wide Web. Because Web pages can change without notice, what you see might not always match what's described in the lab. You might have to search the Web to find the best match for links in steps. When in doubt, check with your instructor.

Lab 1.1 Becoming Familiar with the Squid Proxy Server

Objectives

The goal of this lab is to become familiar with a useful open-source software package that runs on Linux. The Squid proxy server is a great example of a high-quality software package that's free and well supported and runs on many different hardware and software platforms.

Materials Required

This lab requires the following:

- An Internet connection
- A Web browser

Estimated completion time: 30 minutes

Activity Background

There are thousands of software packages you can run on Linux. The Squid proxy server is a particularly useful one because it can substantially reduce the Internet bandwidth required for Web browsing and improve the performance of FTP file transfers. Squid serves as a good example of the support available for open-source software.

Activity

1. Start your Web browser.
2. Type **http://www.squid-cache.org** in the address bar, and then press **Enter** to display the Squid Web Proxy Cache page.
3. Click the **About Squid** link at the left. Spend some time reviewing the information. Next, click the **Why Squid?** link and read why many Internet providers use Squid.
4. Click the **Squid Deployment Case-Studies** link at the left. Click the **Wikipedia Squid Deployment** link, and spend some time reading about how WikiMedia uses Squid.
5. Click the **FAQ** link at the left, and then click the **/AboutSquid** link. Browse through the page, and notice the plethora of operating systems Squid supports.
6. If you're continuing to the next lab, leave your Web browser open; otherwise, close it.

Review Questions

1. Squid can cache which of the following protocols? (Choose all that apply.)
   a. HTTP
   b. SMTP
   c. FTP
   d. SSH

2. Squid can run only on Linux. True or False?

3. Squid performs best when your computer has a lot of memory. True or False?

4. Squid uses hard disk space as its secondary cache. True or False?

5. Technically, Squid is which of the following?
   a. Web browser cache
   b. Internet object cache
   c. TCP port stretcher
   d. Processor L3 cache

Lab 1.2 Exploring Different Linux Distributions

Objectives

There are dozens of Linux distributions, often referred to as "distros." In this lab, you visit the DistroWatch.com site to review some well-known distros and read about their unique features.

Materials Required

This lab requires the following:

- An Internet connection
- A Web browser

Estimated completion time: 30 minutes

Activity

1. Start your Web browser, if necessary.

2. Type **distrowatch.com** in the address bar and press **Enter**.

3. Click the **Distribution** list arrow. In the list of distributions you can search, click **Fedora**, and then click **Refresh**. Fedora 13 comes with this book, and as you can see, there are a number of releases after this version. Scroll down to Fedora 13 and read about some interesting features included in the Fedora 13 release.

4. Scroll back up to the top. This time, click **Ubuntu** in the Distribution list box, and then click **Refresh**. Find the Distribution Release: Ubuntu 12.04 article, and click the **features page** link. Read about some features available in what many consider one of the better Linux desktop/laptop distros.

5. Click your browser's **Back** button until you get back to the DistroWatch.com page. Click **Red Hat** in the Distribution list box, and then click **Refresh**. Find the Distribution Release: Red Hat Enterprise Linux 5.8 article. Read the description of this release and compare it with the Ubuntu description. Can you tell which distro is marketed as a server OS and which is marketed as a desktop OS?

6. Read about other well-known distros, such as CentOS, Knoppix, and openSUSE. If you're continuing to the next lab, leave your Web browser open; otherwise, close it.

Review Questions

1. There are many distributions of the Linux OS for which of the following reasons?

   a.   It's proprietary software.

   b.   Microsoft allows any vendor to ship its own version as long as it contains a Microsoft logo.

   c.   It's open-source software.

   d.   The licensing costs are only about $100 per distribution.

2. Fedora is the community distribution of which commercial product?

   a.   Ubuntu

   b.   OpenSUSE

   c.   CentOS

   d.   Red Hat Enterprise

3. Ubuntu distributions are targeted mainly toward enterprise-level server applications. True or False?

4. According to the DistroWatch Web site, roughly how many Linux distributions are available?

   a.   About 10

   b.   Well over 100

   c.   About two dozen

   d.   Around 50

5. Knoppix is a live CD/DVD distribution of Linux. True or False?

Lab 1.3 Exploring Open-Source Web Server Use

Objectives

The goal of this lab is to help you see the widespread use of open-source Web servers, using a factor that's well understood in the commercial software world—market share. In this lab, you conduct research to discover the percentage of Web servers running the three most popular Web server packages: Apache, Microsoft IIS, and Oracle iPlanet.

Materials Required

This lab requires the following:

- An Internet connection
- A Web browser

Estimated completion time: 20 minutes

Activity

1. Start your Web browser.

2. Type **http://news.netcraft.com/archives/web_server_survey.html** in the address bar, and then press **Enter** to display the Netcraft Web Server Survey site. This site has a graph showing the market share for the most popular Web servers. Note that Apache leads the pack by a wide margin.

 One factor with a major effect on the Netcraft survey results is "virtual hosting," a feature that allows a single Web server to host many Internet sites or URLs. In the Netcraft survey, an ISP running a single Web server with 5000 virtual hosts is seen as 5000 Web servers, not a single Web server.

3. Type **http://www.biznix.org/surveys/websrv.html** in the address bar, and then press **Enter** to see the results of a Web server survey conducted by BizNix, a user group in Portland, Oregon. This survey is limited to well-defined categories of Web server users, such as big companies, government agencies, and military departments. It minimizes the effects of virtual hosting to get a more accurate picture of Web server popularity. The results are quite a bit different from the Netcraft survey results.

4. Compare the results of the BizNix and Netcraft surveys. How are they similar? How do they differ? Note the BizNix survey's conclusion that Microsoft IIS popularity is a U.S. phenomenon.

5. If you're continuing to the next lab, leave your Web browser open; otherwise, close it.

Review Questions

1. Why might the Netcraft survey not be an accurate way of determining the number of Apache Web servers on the Internet?

   a. There's no way to know what software a Web server is using.

   b. A Web server could be using virtual hosting that allows one physical Web server to appear as numerous Web servers.

   c. Web server administrators might have servers masquerade as other types of software to improve compatibility between their servers and popular Web browsers.

2. Why are the BizNix results likely to give a more accurate picture of Apache market share?

   a. The big companies, government agencies, and military departments surveyed are less likely to use virtual hosting.

   b. The BizNix survey knows when a Web server is lying about the software it's using.

   c. The BizNix survey knows when Web servers have had their software upgraded.

3. The percentage of Apache use by big companies in the United States is the same as big companies in other parts of the world. True or False?

4. The BizNix survey shows that Microsoft IIS Web server's popularity is the same in all countries. True or False?

Lab 1.4 Seeing How Linux and Windows Can Be Integrated

Objectives

The goal of this lab is to help you become aware of the many ways Linux and Windows computers can be integrated.

Materials Required

This lab requires the following:

- An Internet connection
- A Web browser

Estimated completion time: 30 minutes

Activity

1. Start your Web browser. Type **http://www.samba.org** in the address bar and press **Enter**.

2. On the Samba home page, click the **think Samba** link, and then click the **The Official Samba HOWTO** link. Review some of the documentation. (Samba is one of the best documented open-source software projects.) You'll find that when you run Samba on your Linux computer, it becomes a file and print server compatible with Windows computers.

3. Type **http://www.winehq.org** in the address bar and press **Enter** to go to the Web site for Wine, a project that allows running Windows programs on a Linux computer.

4. Click the **About** link to go to the About Wine Web page, which states that the first stable release of Wine was in 2008, and it's still under active development. It has been for many years, and its status is not likely to change soon. However, many people use Wine with various levels of success.

5. Under "Open Source and User Driven," click the **Application Database** link. This page tells you which Windows applications work well in a Wine environment and which don't.

6. Type **http://www.vmware.com** in the address bar and press **Enter** to go to the site for VMware, a commercial product that enables you to run Windows programs on a Linux computer or vice versa. VMware's approach is different from Wine's. It requires installing a Windows OS on a virtual machine running on your Linux computer. (The site explains the concept of a virtual machine.) When you run Windows programs on a virtual machine, they're actually running in Windows and should, therefore, run correctly. VMware is one of the best ways to run Windows applications on a Linux computer.

7. Type **http://www.rdesktop.org** in the address bar and press **Enter** to go to the Web site for rdesktop, a Windows Terminal Server client for Linux. Using rdesktop, you can run

1

Windows programs on your Windows Terminal Server machine but have Linux operate your screen, keyboard, and mouse. Your Windows programs are running on a Windows client, but you're using a Linux computer.

8. If you're continuing to the next lab, leave your Web browser open; otherwise, close it.

All the Windows-Linux integration solutions you've seen in this lab can be used separately or in combination. There are many ways to introduce open-source software and Linux into your company without sacrificing Windows features. With these integration solutions, you can run newer Linux applications on the same computers and networks that are running Windows applications.

Review Questions

1. On which of the following operating systems would you *not* expect to find Samba running? (Choose all that apply.)

   a.   Linux

   b.   FreeBSD

   c.   Windows

   d.   NetWare

2. A Samba server is what kind of server?

   a.   SMTP server

   b.   File and print server

   c.   Application server

   d.   DNS server

3. Using Samba, a Linux computer can access files on a Windows computer. True or False?

4. Wine requires installing a Windows OS on your Linux computer. True or False?

5. The rdesktop program allows you to run a Windows application on a Windows Terminal Server client but use your Linux computer's screen, keyboard, and mouse. True or False?

Lab 1.5 Investigating Linux Security

Objectives

The goal of this lab is to show you why open-source software, including Linux, tends to be more secure than other operating systems.

Materials Required

This lab requires the following:

- An Internet connection
- A Web browser

Estimated completion time: 30 minutes

Activity

1. Start your Web browser.

2. Type **http://www.linuxsecurity.com** in the address bar and press **Enter** to see a Web page on Linux security matters. The page contents change frequently, so feel free to explore. Notice that you're cautioned about potential security holes in software, warned to use secure protocols (such as SSH) instead of unsecured ones (such as Telnet), and so forth. The emphasis is on how to avoid security problems and attacks. Linux software updates and patches are usually available before Web sites are attacked, unlike the typical situation with commercial software (with updates and patches becoming available only after sites are attacked).

3. Click the **HOWTOs** link near the top. Then click the **Secure my firewall** link to go to a list of articles and Web sites on Linux firewalls. The Linux OS has a built-in firewall. You just need to configure it—and that can be challenging if you don't understand protocols such as IP, TCP, and UDP. The resources on this page help you configure the firewall by giving you instructions or supplying software (such as scripts) that makes it easier.

 Because Linux has a built-in firewall, you can deploy a firewall at no extra cost on any Linux computer.

4. Type **http://www.ietf.org/rfc/rfc2137.txt** in the address bar and press **Enter**. You're looking at a Request for Comment (RFC), published by the Internet Engineering Task Force (IETF) to describe an Internet standard. (The IETF is the caretaker of the Internet, and its focus is on security issues and protecting the Internet from attack.) This document's content is detailed and technical and might be beyond your comprehension, but you're focusing on how the IETF handles security concerns.

5. Scroll down until you see the section "Security Considerations," and read these paragraphs. Most IETF RFCs have a security section. What do IETF RFCs have to do with Linux? Plenty. Designers of Linux and other open-source software use open protocols and standards, such as IETF RFCs, to be compatible with other software. The only time designers use proprietary protocols is when they're designing software to integrate with a vendor's product, as with the Samba project.

6. Type **http://www.nsa.gov/research/selinux** in the address bar and press **Enter** to see the SELinux (stands for "security enhanced Linux") site. SELinux, created by the U.S. National Security Agency (NSA), adds extensions to Linux to make it less vulnerable to break-ins. Even if a Linux computer is attacked, SELinux severely limits the attacker's ability to do anything on the computer. Attacks common in the Windows world, such as Code Red and Nimda, are rare in the Linux world, even without SELinux. With SELinux, these attacks are highly unlikely.

7. Exit your browser, and close any open windows.

Review Questions

1. Which of the following statements about Linux security is correct?

    a. Linux e-mail programs are easy targets for viruses, as is Microsoft Outlook.

    b. Linux has a built-in firewall you can use to secure any Linux computer, but you must configure it.

    c. Linux Web browsers can't use SSL to access secure Web pages.

    d. Sometimes Web browsers can't connect to Apache Web servers because Apache doesn't follow open standards for security.

2. There are as many virus scanner programs for Linux as there are for Windows. True or False?

3. Explain why Linux is more secure than Windows, even though there are numerous software updates and patches for Windows-based software.

4. Explain why open protocols, such as those documented in IETF RFCs, tend to have fewer security issues than proprietary protocols.

5. If you use the NSA's SELinux, in the unlikely event of a successful attack, the attacker is prevented from causing major damage to your Linux computer. True or False?

LINUX INSTALLATION AND USE

Labs included in this chapter

- Lab 2.1 Booting Linux from a CD/DVD

- Lab 2.2 Testing Your Computer's Memory

- Lab 2.3 Researching Hardware Support

- Lab 2.4 Locating the Kernel File

- Lab 2.5 Seeing Everything as a File

- Lab 2.6 Giving Shutdown Notification

CompTIA Linux+ Exam Objectives

Objective		Lab
101.1	Determine and configure hardware settings	2.1, 2.2, 2.3
101.2	Boot the system	2.1, 2.4
101.3	Change runlevels and shut down or reboot system	2.6
103.1	Work on the command line	2.1, 2.5, 2.6

Lab 2.1 Booting Linux from a CD/DVD

Objectives

In this lab, you download and install Knoppix, a full-featured Linux live distribution. It includes hundreds of applications, such as K-Office and Open Office, which are office suites. Knoppix enables you to boot Linux from a CD/DVD so that you don't have to use any hard disk space. You can run Knoppix on a computer with Windows (or any other OS) installed and all its disk space already allocated.

 Some steps in this activity might differ slightly, depending on the Knoppix version you download.

Materials Required

This lab requires the following:

- A computer with a CD-ROM burner and software installed
- A Web browser and an Internet connection
- A blank CD

Estimated completion time: 45 minutes

Activity

1. Start your Web browser, and go to **http://www.knopper.net/knoppix/index-en.html**. Click the **Download** link, choose a nearby mirror site, and then download the Knoppix .iso file. After it's downloaded, open the file and burn it to a CD. (*Note*: Downloading the file might take a long time, depending on your connection speed; for example, with a DSL connection, the download might take an hour and a half or more.)

2. Make sure your computer supports the minimum requirements specified on the Web site. Read the discussion about creating a swap partition on your hard disk so that you can run graphics with less memory. However, a swap partition isn't required.

3. Boot from the CD. This process might require reconfiguring your computer's BIOS to boot from a CD rather than a hard disk. Refer to your computer's documentation for how to do this reconfiguration.

4. Eventually, the Knoppix menu is displayed. Arrow down to **Shell** and press **Enter**. You'll be logged in as root at the Linux shell prompt.

5. Go to the/proc directory by typing **cd /proc** and pressing **Enter**.

6. Type **ls** and press **Enter**. The filenames and directory names that are displayed in the /proc directory aren't real files, nor do they actually exist on your system's hard disk. The Linux kernel simulates them as a convenient way for you to access information about your system with the familiar ls command.

7. Type **cat cpuinfo** and press **Enter** to see information about the CPU. If the information scrolls off the screen, use the `more cpuinfo` command to pause the output when the screen is filled. You can press the spacebar as needed to view the next page of output. You see a screen that's similar to the following:

```
processor:   0
vendor id:   GenuineIntel
cpu family: 6
model:       42
model name:  Intel® Core™ i7-2600 CPU @ 3.40GHz
stepping:    6
cpu MHz:     3392.359
cache size:  8192 KB
. . .
```

This output tells you that the computer is an Intel Core i7 with an 8 MB cache running at 3.4 GHz, along with other details that might not be important to you.

8. Type **more interrupts** and press **Enter** to see information about interrupt assignments, similar to the following:

```
CPU0
 0:  52       IO-APIC-edge timer
 1:  381      IO-APIC-edge keyboard
 2:  45       IO-APIC-edge cascade
 6:  5        IO-APIC-edge floppy
 8:  1        IO-APIC-edge rtc
11: 2424      IO-APIC-edge eth0, SiS 7018 PCI Audio
12: 2542269   IO-APIC-edge PS/2 Mouse
 . . .
```

This output shows the hardware interrupts in your computer and what devices use these interrupts. This example shows that this computer has the usual hardware plus a LAN adapter (eth0) and an audio device on interrupt 11. It also has a mouse on interrupt 12.

9. Type **more ioports** and press **Enter** to see information about the I/O ports your computer's devices use.

10. Type **cat dma** and press **Enter** to show devices that use DMA channels.

11. Type **exit** and press **Enter** to go back to the menu. To shut down your system, scroll down to the **Shutdown** command on the menu and press **Enter**. Press **Enter** again and press **y** to verify.

Both the cat and more commands display a text file's contents. However, cat displays it all at once, allowing contents to scroll off the screen, and more pauses the output as each screen fills. Pressing the spacebar displays the next screen, and pressing any other key stops the display.

Review Questions

1. To run Knoppix, your computer must be capable of which of the following?

   a. Booting from a 3.5-inch disk

   b. Booting from a CD

   c. Booting from a hard disk

   d. Booting from a Web site

2. Knoppix requires creating a Linux swap partition on your computer's hard disk. True or False?

3. If you have Windows installed on your computer, you can't run Knoppix. True or False?

4. The files in the `/proc` directory take up space on your computer's hard disk. True or False?

5. What command do you use to get information about your system's processor?

Lab 2.2 Testing Your Computer's Memory

Objectives

In this lab, you download and install a memory-testing program called Memtest86. It runs on any Intel-based computer and doesn't require installing an OS. You download a bootable ISO file and burn it to a CD.

Materials Required

This lab requires the following:

- A computer running Windows (any version) or Linux with CD-burning software
- An Internet connection and a Web browser
- A blank CD

Estimated completion time: 40 minutes

Activity Background

Any OS fails to work reliably if the computer's memory is faulty, and Linux is no exception. Before you install Linux, it's a good idea to check your computer's memory. The memory test that's conducted each time you start your computer isn't a comprehensive one, and some memory problems might escape detection. It's best to run a comprehensive memory-testing program, such as Memtest86.

Activity

1. Start your computer. Start your Web browser, if necessary, and go to **www.memtest86.com**. Click the **Free Download** link, and then click the **Version 4.0a** link (or the most recent nonserver version available). Click the **Linux (gzip) ISO image for creating bootable CD** or **Windows (zip) ISO image for creating bootable CD** link (depending on whether you're running Windows or Linux). After the file has downloaded, unzip it and burn it to a blank CD.

2. While the file is downloading and burning, click the **Change Log** link, and read about some recent enhancements to Memtest86.

3. After you have burned the CD, boot your system from it. The Memtest86 program should load in a few seconds and begin running immediately.

4. After the program runs a few seconds, the screen should look similar to the following, but the numbers displayed will be different:

```
Memtest-86 v 4.0a        |   Intel® Core™ i7-2600 CPU @ 3.40 GHz
CPU Clk: 3392 MHz        |   Pass 40% ############
L1 Cache 64K 113072 MB/s |   Test 30% ############
L2 Cache 256K 55609 MB/s |   Test #9
L3 Cache 8192K 5655362 MB/s |  Testing 260K - 256M
Memory 256M 23721 MB/s   |   Pattern: bffffffffffff
```

2

This test tells you how much memory is installed. The fifth line, "Testing 260K - 256M," shows the range of memory being tested. It also computes and displays the speed of your processor's L1, L2, and L3 caches. The sixth line shows the speed of your computer's main memory (23721 MB/s, in this example). Normally, the Memtest86 program runs 11 memory tests. The fourth line shows the current test number (Test #9, in this example).

When all tests are finished, it means one "pass" has been completed, and the tests repeat. The pass number is displayed in the last line of output (not shown in this example). Memtest86 continues to run test passes until you exit the program. Press **c** while the program is running to display a menu for controlling Memtest86's operation.

5. Type **0** to exit this menu. Press **Esc** to exit Memtest86, and then remove the CD from the drive. You can learn more about the configuration options in Step 4 by reading the information at *www.memtest86.com*.

6. Leave your system running for the next lab.

TIP   Linux has an interesting capability to use faulty memory modules by bypassing these memory locations. If you discover memory errors, you can tell Linux to avoid using these areas of memory instead of replacing the memory modules. This feature is called BadRAM. To learn more, go to *http://aplawrence.com/Drag/B1237.html*.

Review Questions

1. Running Memtest86 requires installing Linux on the computer first. True or False?

2. Memtest86 stops testing after how many passes?

   a. 1

   b. 2

   c. 8

   d. 16

   e. Until you exit

3. Memtest86 tests only main memory, not the processor's cache. True or False?

4. Memtest86 performs tests only on single-core CPUs. True or False?

5. Linux can be configured to work with memory that has errors. True or False?

Lab 2.3 Researching Hardware Support

Objectives

In this lab, you do research to see how well Linux supports the latest hardware, such as USB 3.0 and High-Definition Multimedia Interface (HDMI). You can find this hardware on many new computers.

Materials Required

This lab requires the following:

- A computer running Windows (any version) or Linux
- An Internet connection and a Web browser

Estimated completion time: 30 minutes

Activity Background

Say you want to purchase a new computer that works with Linux. The computer you're considering has USB 3.0 ports and an HDMI port, and you want to find out whether Linux supports these technologies.

Activity

1. Start your Web browser, if necessary, and go to **www.google.com**. Enter **linux usb 3.0** in the search box and click the **Google Search** button or press **Enter**. Notice the large number of sites returned in the search results.

2. Click **Linux and USB 3.0 - No Bragging Rights for Windows**. If you can't find this article, go to **http://www.linuxplanet.com/linuxplanet/reports/6956/1**.

3. Read the article to learn more about USB 3.0 and find out when the Linux OS started supporting USB 3.0.

4. Next, use Google to search for **Linux HDMI**.

5. Click the **How to Setup HDMI Digital Playback in Linux** link. Read the article about how to use a Linux system to output high-definition video to a TV.

6. Close your Web browser, and leave your system running for the next lab.

Review Questions

1. FireWire (IEEE 1394) is faster than USB 2.0. True or False?

2. What is the maximum speed of USB 2.0?

   a.   1 Mbps (megabits per second)

   b.   12 Mbps

   c.   480 Mbps

   d.   5 Gbps (gigabits per second)

3. What is the maximum speed of USB 3.0?

    a. 1 Mbps

    b. 12 Mbps

    c. 480 Mbps

    d. 5 Gbps

4. HDMI ports are used to transfer files to external drives. True or False?

5. When did Linux start supporting USB 3.0?

    a. May 2004

    b. September 2009

    c. January 2011

    d. Linux doesn't support USB 3.0.

Lab 2.4 Locating the Kernel File

Objectives

The goal of this lab is to learn how to find the kernel file on your hard disk.

Materials Required

This lab requires the following:

- A computer running Fedora 13 Linux

Estimated completion time: 10 minutes

Activity Background

The Linux kernel is typically stored on the hard disk in an ordinary file, which allows your system to boot quickly. You should know where this file is located because you might want to create a boot disk, or you might need to modify your boot loader (LILO or GRUB) configuration file. Knowing the kernel file's name and location is necessary for either task.

Activity

1. Boot your Linux computer. If it's displaying a graphical desktop, such as GNOME or KDE, switch to a command-line terminal (`tty`) by pressing **Ctrl+Alt+F2**. Log in as root.

2. Most Linux distributions place the kernel file in the `/boot` directory, but it can be located anywhere. Some distributions place it in the root (`/`) directory. Go to the `/boot` directory by typing **cd /boot** and pressing Enter.

3. Display the files in the `/boot` directory by typing **ls -loS** and pressing **Enter**. This command specifies displaying a long directory listing (`-l`), suppressing the display of the group (`o`) owner, and reverse-sorting the files by size (`S`). Remember that Linux commands are case sensitive, so you must use the correct lowercase or uppercase letters. The file starting with `vmlinuz` is most likely the kernel file. In Fedora 13, the kernel file is `vmlinuz-2.6.33.3-85.fc13.i686.PAE`.

4. Your system might have more than one kernel file. If so, how can you tell which one is being used to boot the system? Look at the boot loader configuration file. For a Fedora 13 system, the boot loader file is normally `/etc/grub.conf`. Display its contents by typing **cat /etc/grub.conf** and pressing **Enter**. When the file is displayed, ignore any comments (lines starting with the # symbol). Here's an example of what the file contains (minus comments):

```
default=0
timeout=10
splashimage=(hd0,0)/grub/splash.xpm.gz
hiddenmenu
title Fedora (2.6.33.3-85.fc13.i686.PAE)
root (hd0,0)
kernel /boot/vmlinuz-2.6.33.3-85.fc13.i686.PAE
    initrd /initramfs-2.6.33.3-85.fc13.i686.PAE.img
```

The seventh line identifies the kernel file as `/boot/vmlinuz-2.6.33.3-85.fc13.i686.PAE`. If GRUB is configured to boot from more than one kernel, you see two title sections in the `/etc/grub.conf` file, similar to the preceding example.

5. Your system might be using the LILO boot loader rather than GRUB. If so, the configuration file is `/etc/lilo.conf`. To display its contents, type **cat /etc/lilo.conf** and press **Enter**.

6. Linux kernels aren't required to have certain filenames. Any name can be used. You can name the kernel file `mykernel` or `mycolonel`, for example. So if you can't tell a kernel file by its name, how can you tell whether a file is a kernel file? It's easy: You use the `file` command. Type **file *name*** (replacing *name* with the name of the file you want to test) and press **Enter**. For example, on a Fedora 13 system, type **file /boot/vmlinuz-*** and press **Enter**. The output `/boot/vmlinuz-2.6.33.3-85.fc13.i686.PAE: Linux kernel x86 boot executable...` is displayed. The * character in the preceding command is used to issue the `file` command on any file with a name beginning with `/boot/vmlinuz-`.

7. If you're continuing to the next lab, leave your computer on; otherwise, go back to the graphical interface by pressing **Alt+F1** or shut down the computer.

Review Questions

1. Most Linux distributions place the kernel file in which directory?

   a. root (/) directory

   b. `/boot`

   c. `/etc`

   d. `/loader`

2. If there's more than one kernel file on your system, how can you tell which one the system uses to boot Linux?

3. Which are the two most widely used boot loader programs in Linux?

   a. `rpm` and `dpkg`

   b. `file` and `ls`

   c. LILO and GRUB

   d. `/` and `/boot`

4. If you're using the LILO boot loader, what is its configuration file?

    a.   `/boot/lilo`

    b.   `/boot/lilo.conf`

    c.   `/etc/lilo`

    d.   `/etc/lilo.conf`

5. Which command tells you whether a file is a kernel file?

    a.   `kernel`

    b.   `file`

    c.   `ls -k`

    d.   `which`

Lab 2.5 Seeing Everything as a File

Objectives

The goal of this lab is to show you that Linux, like UNIX, is file oriented in its behavior and treats all (or most) devices as though they're files.

Materials Required

This lab requires the following:

- A computer running Fedora 13 Linux

Estimated completion time: 15 minutes

Activity Background

Chapter 2 in the textbook introduces the concept of terminals and shows you how to move between them with Alt or Ctrl+Alt key sequences. These terminals are devices, and most or all devices in Linux can be treated as files. This activity shows you how to read from them and write to them. The practical applications for writing strings (or other data) to other terminal screens might not seem clear now, but you'll appreciate this flexibility as you gain more experience with Linux. The ability to send output to specific terminal screens is particularly useful when you write shell scripts and configure your system for logging. These topics are covered in later chapters.

Activity

1. Start your Linux system and log in, if necessary. If your computer is displaying a graphical desktop, press **Ctrl+Alt+F2** to go to a command prompt.

2. Log in as root.

3. To send the string "Hello from tty2" to the `tty5` device, type **echo "Hello from tty2" > /dev/tty5** and press **Enter**.

The letters "tty" are an abbreviation for teletype, an obsolete electromechanical terminal used in the early days of computing. Linux and UNIX use this abbreviation to refer to modern consoles. To refer to a `tty`, you must precede the name with `/dev/`.

4. Switch to `tty5` by pressing **Alt+F5**. You should see the string "Hello from tty2" on the `tty5` terminal screen. Note that even though the message you sent to `tty5` is next to the login prompt, the login prompt didn't register the input as an attempt to log in; no running programs in a terminal register text messages sent to it as input. Login to `tty5` as root.

5. From `tty5`, write to `tty2` by typing **echo "Hello yourself " > /dev/tty2** and pressing **Enter**.

6. Press **Alt+F2** to go back to `tty2`. Notice that the string "Hello yourself " is displayed.

7. So far, you've simply sent text messages to other terminals. You can also copy one device to another. One interesting device is the random number generator, called `/dev/urandom`. Copy random numbers to `tty5` by typing **cat /dev/urandom > /dev/tty5** and pressing **Enter**. You'll likely hear the computer's speaker beeping, which is normal.

8. Switch to `tty5` by pressing **Alt+F5**. The screen should be rapidly filling with characters and scrolling as random characters are displayed.

The random numbers from `/dev/urandom` aren't displayed as normal decimal numbers. They're binary numbers that the `tty` interprets as characters.

9. Stop the random numbers from being displayed on `tty5` by switching back to `tty2` and pressing **Ctrl+C**.

10. If you're continuing to the next lab, leave your computer on; otherwise, go back to the graphical interface by pressing **Alt+F1** or shut down the computer.

Review Questions

1. Which of the following is the correct way to refer to terminals in Linux commands?

   a. `tty5`

   b. `device:tty5`

   c. `/dev/tty5`

   d. `tty:5`

2. If you send a string to a `tty` being used by a program, is the program aware that you wrote to its screen?

3. Suppose a device called `/dev/dice` produces random numbers between 1 and 6 (simulating the role of a die). What command do you use to display these numbers to `tty6`?

   a. `cat /dev/dice > /dev/tty6`

   b. `cat /dev/dice > tty6`

   c. `cat dice > /dev/tty6`

   d. `cat dice > tty6`

4. Write the correct command to send the contents of the GRUB boot loader configuration file to `tty5`.

Lab 2.6 Giving Shutdown Notification

Objectives

The goal of this lab is to learn how to shut down a Linux system so that other users are notified.

Materials Required

This lab requires the following:

- A computer running Fedora 13 Linux

Estimated completion time: 30 minutes

Activity Background

When Linux computers are networked and one computer's resources are being used by others, it's useful to notify all users when the system is being shut down so that they have a chance to save their data and exit applications before the shutdown. You can use the Linux `shutdown` command to specify a notification message and send it to users automatically.

Activity

1. If your computer is displaying a graphical desktop, press **Ctrl+Alt+F2** to go to a command prompt.

2. Log in as root.

3. Tell Linux to shut down five minutes from now by typing **shutdown -h +5 The system is going down** and pressing **Enter**. You see the following messages onscreen:

   ```
   The system is going down for system halt in 5 minutes!!
   The system is going down
   ```

4. Wait about four minutes, and you see these additional lines displayed onscreen:

   ```
   Broadcast message from root (tty2) Mon Aug 5 08:48:36 2013...
   The system is going down for system halt in 1 minute !!
   The system is going down
   ```

   The system is warning you that it will be shutting down in one minute.

5. Press **Ctrl+C** to abort the shutdown.

6. Type **shutdown -h 5 The system is going down** again and press **Enter**. You see the same messages you saw in Step 3.

7. Next, go to `tty5` by pressing **Alt+F5**. Log in as root. After entering your password, in a minute or so you see a message similar to this:

   ```
   The system is going down for halt in 4 minutes!
   The system is going down again.
   ```

8. Go back to `tty2` by pressing **Alt+F2**. Press **Ctrl+C** to abort the shutdown.

9. Review the options for the shutdown command by typing **shutdown --help | more** and pressing **Enter**. Note that you can cancel a pending shutdown. Press the spacebar to cancel the more command.

10. Type **shutdown -h 5 Close all running programs and log off** and press **Enter**.

11. Change to tty5. Log out by typing **exit** and pressing **Enter**, and then log in as a regular user. Wait for the shutdown warning.

12. Type **shutdown -c** and press **Enter**. Notice that only the root user can issue the shutdown command. Log out, and then log in as root. Type **shutdown -c** and press **Enter**.

13. Switch back to tty2 to see that the shutdown has been canceled.

14. Shut down your system.

Review Questions

1. When using the shutdown command, the only option is to halt the system. True or False?

2. By default, any user can cancel a shutdown, but only the root user can actually shut the system down. True or False?

3. Which command shuts the system down and reboots immediately?

    a.   shutdown -P 0

    b.   shutdown -r now

    c.   shutdown -r

    d.   shutdown -P -0

4. Write the command to send this shutdown warning message: "The system is going down for maintenance in 2 minutes! You really need to log off now!" However, don't actually shut the system down.

5. Write the command to cancel a pending shutdown.

CHAPTER 3

EXPLORING LINUX FILE SYSTEMS

Labs included in this chapter

- Lab 3.1 Creating Complex Functions with Simple Commands
- Lab 3.2 Performing Complex Searches
- Lab 3.3 Doing More with Less
- Lab 3.4 Displaying Binary Data
- Lab 3.5 Working with Unusual File and Directory Names

CompTIA Linux+ Exam Objectives

Objective		Lab
103.1	Work on the command line	3.1, 3.2, 3.5
103.2	Process text streams using filters	3.1, 3.2
103.3	Perform basic file management	3.4, 3.5
103.4	Use streams, pipes, and redirects	3.2, 3.3
103.7	Search text files using regular expressions	3.2

Lab 3.1 Creating Complex Functions with Simple Commands

Objectives

The goal of this lab is to create complex functions by stringing two or more simple Linux commands together. Linux commands can be connected by using pipes, which send one command's output to another command as input. After completing this lab, you'll be able to do the following:

- Pause the display of data at each full screen
- Display text strings embedded in binary data
- Filter a data stream based on a word

Materials Required

This lab requires the following:

- A computer running Fedora 13 Linux

Estimated completion time: 15 minutes

Activity

1. Switch to a command-line terminal (`tty2`) by pressing **Ctrl+Alt+F2**, and log in to the terminal as the root user.

2. This lab uses the `bash` man page file, which is in the `/usr/share/man/man1` directory in Fedora. You can find man pages in a subdirectory of `/usr/share/man`, with the number in the subdirectory referring to a man page section. To find the exact filename for the man page, type **ls -l /usr/share/man/man1/bash*** and press **Enter**. You should see something similar to the following (although more files might be listed):

   ```
   -rw-r—r-- 1 root root 64921 Mar 11 03:19 bash.1.gz
   ```

3. The `bash` man page file is compressed, so you have to uncompress it. Type **gunzip /usr/share/man/man1/bash.1.gz** and press **Enter**. The file should now be uncompressed and is called `bash.1`. (The `gunzip` command removes the `.gz` file extension after the file is uncompressed.)

4. The `bash.1` file is a plain text file, so you read it with text-based commands, such as `cat`, `more`, and `less`. First, make the `/usr/share/man/man1` directory your current directory by typing **cd /usr/share/man/man1** and pressing **Enter**.

5. Type **cat bash.1** and press **Enter**. Because the file is large, the screen might scroll, but you can stop the scrolling by pressing **Ctrl+C**.

6. Because the screen scrolls faster than you can read, use a command such as `more` to display the text one page at a time and then pause until you press a key to display the next page. Type **more bash.1** and press **Enter** to see the first page of text.

7. Press any key to see the next page of text. If you don't want to view the entire file, you can exit `more` and get back to the command prompt by typing **q**.

8. The `more` command doesn't allow you to go back in the file to see text on previous pages. To do that, you use the `less` command. Type **less bash.1** and press **Enter**. To move forward and backward in the file, press the **Page Down** and **Page Up** keys. When you have finished, press **q** to exit the `less` command.

9. You can use the `grep` command to display only lines containing certain words. Type **cat bash.1 | grep input** and press **Enter**. In this command, you're telling `grep` to display only lines containing the string `input`.

10. You can also use the `more` or `less` commands with `grep`. Type **cat bash.1 | grep input | more** and press **Enter**. Notice that the screen stops after filling the page. Exit the `more` command by pressing **q**.

11. Type **logout** and press **Enter** to log out of the system, and press **Ctrl+Alt+F1** to go back to the graphical screen.

Review Questions

1. In which directory are man pages located in Fedora Linux?

   a. `/etc/man`

   b. `/var/man`

   c. `/usr/sbin/man`

   d. `/usr/share/man`

2. Man pages are normally stored in compressed form. True or False?

3. If you want to find certain strings in a file, which command do you use to filter the file's contents?

   a. `ls`

   b. `grep`

   c. `strings`

   d. `less`

4. Which command do you use to display only one page of text at a time?

   a. `ls`

   b. `cat`

   c. `grep`

   d. `more`

5. The `less` command functions much like which of the following?

   a. `ls`

   b. `more`

   c. `grep`

   d. `cat`

Lab 3.2 Performing Complex Searches

Objectives

The goal of this lab is to learn how regular expressions and the grep command can be used for complex searches of documents. Regular expressions are useful when searching for lines in a text file or data stream containing certain strings. Sometimes, however, you need to find lines based on more complex criteria. For example, if you want to extract lines from a file or data stream containing two words that aren't adjacent, creating a regular expression to handle this situation could be difficult. A simple solution is to use two grep filters, one for each word. Any lines passing through both filters contain both words.

Materials Required

This lab requires the following:

- A computer running Fedora 13 Linux

Estimated completion time: 15 minutes

Activity

1. Switch to a command-line terminal (tty2) by pressing **Ctrl+Alt+F2**, and log in to the terminal as the root user.

2. Move to the /usr/share/man/man1 directory by typing **cd /usr/share/man/man1** and pressing **Enter**.

3. Type **cat bash.1 | grep display | less** and press **Enter**. The word "display" in lowercase letters is shown on all lines. Press **q** to quit.

4. Type **cat bash.1 | grep Display | less** and press **Enter**. The word "Display," starting with an uppercase letter, is shown on all lines. Press **q** to quit.

5. Searches with grep are usually case sensitive, but you can use the -i option for searches that aren't case-sensitive. Type **cat bash.1 | grep -i display | less** and press **Enter**. The output contains both "display" and "Display." Press **q** to quit.

6. To make the search more complex, you can search for more than one word. Type **cat bash.1 | grep -i display | grep history** and press **Enter**. There's no need to pipe the output to the less filter because it's unlikely that more than a few lines will match. You see a few lines containing "display" (for the search that's not case sensitive) and "history" (for the case-sensitive search).

7. You can also use grep to search for regular expressions. To try searching for a simple regular expression, type **cat bash.1 | grep ^When | grep script** and press **Enter**. The caret (^) indicates searching for the word "When" at the start of a line. You see a line containing "When" at the start of the line and "script" elsewhere in the line.

8. You uncompressed the bash.1 file in Step 3 of Lab 3.1. To restore it to its compressed form, type **gzip bash.1** and press **Enter**.

9. Type **ls bash*** and press **Enter**. You see a list of files starting with "bash," including the bash.1.gz file you just created with the gzip command.

10. Type **logout** and press **Enter** to log out of the system, and press **Ctrl+Alt+F1** to go back to the graphical screen.

Review Questions

1. The `grep` command is usually case sensitive. True or False?

2. Which command do you use to search for strings and ignore the letter case?

   a. `ls`

   b. `ls -l`

   c. `grep`

   d. `grep -i`

3. The `grep` command can search for literal strings or regular expressions. True or False?

4. You can usually avoid complex regular expressions by using two or more `grep` commands piped to one another. True or False?

5. Linux restricts you to piping only two commands together, such as `ls|more`. You can't have more than one pipe, as in `ls|sort|more`. True or False?

Lab 3.3 Doing More with Less

Objectives

The goal of this lab is to learn that the `less` command has numerous options and interactive features for moving through text files.

Materials Required

This lab requires the following:

- A computer running Fedora 13 Linux

Estimated completion time: 15 minutes

Activity Background

Most Linux distributions include an English word list that system utilities or applications can use. This word list is a plain text file called `words` in the `/usr/share/dict` directory; it has one word per line and is alphabetized. You use this file for this lab.

Activity

1. Switch to a command-line terminal (`tty2`) by pressing **Ctrl+Alt+F2**, and log in to the terminal with any username.

2. Type **cd /usr/share/dict** and press **Enter**.

3. To display the `words` file with the `less` command, type **less words** and press **Enter**. You can see that the `words` file has one word per line and is alphabetized.

4. You can move forward (toward the end of the file) and backward (toward the beginning of the file) with the Page Up and Page Down keys. You can also use the spacebar to move forward by one screen and press the b key to move backward by one screen. Press **spacebar** and **b** to try this feature.

5. You can move to the beginning of a file by pressing g and to the end by pressing G. Press **g** to go to the beginning of the `words` file.

6. You can search for a specific word in the words file by using a forward slash, followed by the search term. For example, type **/Monday** and press **Enter**. You should see "Monday" displayed on the top line.

7. Searches are usually case sensitive, so if you search for "monday," "Monday" isn't displayed in the search results. As with the grep command, however, you can do searches that aren't case sensitive by using the -i option. Type -i. A message about "case-insensitive" searching is displayed. When prompted to press the Return key, press **Enter**. Now you can search for words regardless of case.

8. Press **g** to go to the beginning of the file, and then type **/monday** and press **Enter**. You should see "Monday" at the top of the screen.

9. Exit the less command by pressing **q**.

10. Type **logout** and press **Enter** to log out of the system, and press **Ctrl+Alt+F1** to go back to the graphical screen.

Review Questions

1. Which less command do you use to move to the beginning of a file?

   a. g

   b. G

   c. b

   d. B

2. Which less command do you use to move to the end of a file?

   a. g

   b. G

   c. b

   d. B

3. Which key do you press to tell less you want to search?

   a. g

   b. /

   c. spacebar

   d. b

4. Which option do you use to tell less you want to do a search that isn't case sensitive?

   a. G

   b. i

   c. -i

   d. z

Lab 3.4 Displaying Binary Data

Objectives

The goal of this lab is to see how to display binary data files in a variety of formats, such as decimal, hexadecimal, and octal.

Materials Required

This lab requires the following:

- A computer running Fedora 13 Linux

Estimated completion time: 30 minutes

Activity Background

Sometimes you need to search through binary files to find text strings; for example, you might want to know the version number of a program or data file. In this case, viewing the binary file directly might be easier than using the program you'd normally use to open the file. When you want to view binary data, the tools you use sometimes convert it into a form that's convenient to use but sometimes not. One of these tools is the od command, which by default treats the binary data you want to view as a program instead of just binary data. The problem is that it might swap bytes around so that the file's first byte appears after the second byte, the fourth byte appears before the third, and so on. This result is workable if you're a programmer looking at a program dump running on a computer that stores bytes in memory this way, but it's not helpful if you just want to look at simple binary data. In this lab, you work with examples that display bytes in the same order they appear in the file, which is the way most people prefer to see them.

Activity

1. Switch to a command-line terminal (tty2) by pressing **Ctrl+Alt+F2**, and log in to the terminal as the root user.

2. Go to your home directory by typing **cd** and pressing **Enter**.

3. You need a small file containing binary data. To create one by borrowing data from a program file, type **dd count=1 bs=65 if=/bin/sh of=bindata** and press **Enter**. This command creates the bindata file in your home directory. It contains the first 65 bytes of data from the /bin/sh file, which is usually the BASH shell in most Linux distributions. Check the man page for the dd command (man dd) if you want to see exactly how it works.

4. Type **od bindata** and press **Enter**. You see something similar to the following:

```
0000000  042577  043114  000401  000001  000000  000000  000000  000000
0000020  000002  000003  000001  000000  111600  004005  000064  000000
0000040  165464  000007  000000  000000  000064  000040  000006  000050
0000060  000031  000030  000006  000000  000064  000000  100064  004004
0000100  000064
0000101
```

This default format isn't likely to be useful to you. The following steps produce more useful results.

5. To view the file in hexadecimal form, type **od -A x -t x1 bindata** and press **Enter.** The -A x option specifies displaying file offsets in hexadecimal format, and the -t x1 option specifies displaying data in hexadecimal format. The 1 after the x specifies displaying only one byte at a time with a space between each byte. You should see something similar to this:

```
000000  7f  45  4c  46  01  01  01  00  00  00  00  00  00  00  00  00
000010  02  00  03  00  01  00  00  00  80  93  05  08  34  00  00  00
000020  34  eb  07  00  00  00  00  00  34  00  20  00  06  00  28  00
000030  19  00  18  00  06  00  00  00  34  00  00  00  34  80  04  08
000040  34
000041
```

 A file offset is a value that tells you how many bytes from the beginning of the file the data in each line of output begins. In the preceding example, the 000000 value in the first line tells you that the 7f byte of data is at the beginning of the file (0 bytes from the beginning). The 000030 value in the fourth line tells you that the 19th byte of data is 48 (30 hexadecimal) bytes from the beginning of the file.

6. To view the file in decimal format, type **od -A d -t u1 bindata** and press **Enter.** The -A d option specifies displaying a decimal value for the offset, and the -t u1 option specifies displaying data in decimal format, as in this example:

```
0000000  127  69  76  70  1  1  1  0  0  0  0  0  0  0  0  0
0000016  2  0  3  0  1  0  0  0  128  147  5  8  52  0  0  0
0000032  52  235  7  0  0  0  0  0  52  0  32  0  6  0  40  0
0000048  25  0  24  0  6  0  0  0  52  0  0  0  52  128  4  8
0000064  52
0000065
```

7. Sometimes a data file contains plain text but includes nonprintable characters, too. To view these nonprintable characters in their mnemonic form (abbreviations standardized by the ASCII code), type **od -A d -t a bindata** and press **Enter.** You see something similar to the following:

```
0000000  del  E  L  F  soh  soh  soh  nul  nul  nul  nul  nul  nul  nul  nul  nul
0000016  stx  nul  etx  nul  soh  nul  nul  nul  nul  dc3  enq  bs  4  nul  nul  nul
0000032  4  k  bel  nul  nul  nul  nul  nul  4  nul  sp  nul  ack  nul  (  nul
0000048  em  nul  can  nul  ack  nul  nul  nul  4  nul  nul  nul  4  nul  eot  bs
0000064  4
0000065
```

In this example, the first byte is del (a mnemonic), also called rub or rubout in older ASCII versions. The next three bytes are uppercase E, L, and F. The fifth byte is another mnemonic, soh, which stands for "start of heading."

8. Type **logout** and press **Enter** to log out of the system, and press **Ctrl+Alt+F1** to go back to the graphical screen.

Review Questions

1. Which of the following is used to copy a certain number of bytes from one file to another?

   a. `strings`

   b. `dd`

   c. `grep`

   d. `cat`

2. Which option do you use with `od` to specify that you want hexadecimal offsets?

   a. `-A x`

   b. `-a x`

   c. `-a`

   d. `-t x`

3. Which option do you use with `od` to specify that you want hexadecimal data displayed one byte at a time?

   a. `-A x1`

   b. `-a x1`

   c. `-t x1`

   d. `-t o1`

4. Which option do you use with `od` to specify that you want decimal data displayed one byte at a time?

   a. `-A x1`

   b. `-a x1`

   c. `-t u1`

   d. `-t o1`

5. Which option do you use with `od` to specify that you want decimal offsets?

   a. `-A d`

   b. `-a x`

   c. `-t u`

   d. `-t o`

Lab 3.5 Working with Unusual File and Directory Names

Objectives

The goal of this lab is to see how Linux file systems enable you to use almost any file and directory names you like and use any special characters in names.

Materials Required

This lab requires the following:

- A computer running Fedora 13 Linux

Estimated completion time: 20 minutes

Activity Background

If your computing career started with DOS or early Windows versions, you might remember severe restrictions on file and directory names. DOS restricted file and directory names to eight characters with an optional extension of up to three characters. Early Windows versions had the same restriction, but Windows 95 changed it so that names could be up to 256 characters, but there were limitations on the types of characters that were allowed.

Later Windows versions reduced the limitations, but some still remain. Linux has few limitations. You can create names with any characters you like. You just need to realize that some characters might conflict with your system's shell. Although conflicts can result, Linux usually has a way to work around them.

Activity

1. Switch to a command-line terminal (`tty2`) by pressing **Ctrl+Alt+F2**, and log in to the terminal with any username.

2. To change the shell prompt so that you can see your current directory easily, type **PS1="\w:"** and press **Enter**. The prompt now shows the current working directory.

3. Chances are good that the current directory is your home directory. If so, the command prompt should be ~:. If it's not, go to your home directory by typing **cd ~** or **cd** and pressing **Enter**.

4. The tilde (~) represents your home directory. If you want to see the actual directory, type **pwd** and press **Enter**. If you're logged in as root, your home directory is most likely `/root`, although it could be different depending on how the administrator set up the system.

5. Create a directory called `test` below your home directory by typing **mkdir test** and pressing **Enter**. Make it the current directory by typing **cd ~/test** and pressing **Enter**. The command prompt is now ~/test:.

6. Linux includes the `touch` command for creating a file with no contents quickly and easily. Type **touch abc** and press **Enter**, and then type **ls** and press **Enter**. You should see the abc file listed.

7. Type **touch ABC** and press **Enter**, and then type **ls** and press **Enter**. You should see both the abc and ABC files listed. Linux distinguishes between character case, so the abc and ABC files are considered two different files.

8. To use `touch` to create a very long filename, type **touch abcdefghijklmnopqrstuvwxyz1234567890** and press **Enter**. (*Note*: The name must be no longer than 256 characters.) Type **ls** and press **Enter** to see how the long name is displayed. Type **ls -l** and press **Enter** to see how the display differs.

9. To delete this file, take advantage of the BASH completion feature instead of typing the entire filename. To do this, type **rm abcd** and press **Tab**. The command line should display the entire filename. Press **Enter**, and then press **y** and press **Enter** to confirm the deletion. Confirm that the file has been deleted by typing **ls** and pressing **Enter**.

10. Linux, like DOS and Windows, uses a name consisting of a single period (.) to represent the current directory. A name consisting of two periods (. .) represents the parent directory. To see these directories listed, type **ls -a** and press **Enter**.

11. Type **touch** . . . (that's three periods) and press **Enter**. Type **ls -a** and press **Enter**. You see the . . . name in the listing. To verify that it's a file, not a directory, type **ls -al** and press **Enter**. Notice that the . . . entry doesn't start with a d (which stands for "directory").

You can't create file or directory names consisting of only periods in any Windows version.

12. Unusual names, such as . . ., aren't limited to files. Type **mkdir ....** (that's four periods) and press **Enter**. Type **ls -al** and press **Enter** to see that you've created a directory. The entry looks like this:

```
drwxr-xr-x 2 ed users 4096 Jan 24 15:31 ....
```

13. Make . . . . your current directory by typing **cd ....** and pressing **Enter**, and then notice the command prompt.

14. Filenames beginning with a hyphen, such as -n, are allowed but can cause problems because many commands assume the - character is a command-line option. If, for example, you try to use touch to create a file named -n, you get the following error message:

```
touch: invalid option -- n
Try 'touch -- help' for more information.
```

To work around this problem, you need to precede the filename with - - (two dashes), which tells touch no more command-line options follow the - - sequence. Type **touch -- -n** and press **Enter**, and then type **ls -l** and press **Enter**. The following is displayed to confirm that a file was created:

```
-rw-r-r- 1 ed users 0 Jan 24 15:31 -n
```

15. If you want to edit the file with the vi editor, you have a problem if you type vi -n because vi thinks -n is an option indicating not to use a swap file instead of a filename. The solution is using the - - option again so that vi interprets -n as a filename. Type **vi -- -n** and press **Enter** to verify you can edit the file named -n. Press **:q** and then **Enter** to quit vi.

16. If you want to remove the -n file, you have to use the - - trick again. Type **rm -- -n** and press **Enter**, and then press **y** to confirm the deletion. Next, type **ls -al** and press **Enter** to see that the file has been removed.

17. Type **logout** and press **Enter** to log out of the system, and press **Ctrl+Alt+F1** to go back to the graphical screen.

Review Questions

1. Which of the following commands changes the shell prompt to show the current directory?

    a. `prompt $p$g`

    b. `$PROMPT="\w\$"`

    c. `PS1="\w\$"`

    d. `echo $PS1`

2. Which of the following commands brings you to your home directory? (Choose all that apply.)

    a. `cd`

    b. `cd -`

    c. `cd ~`

    d. `cd \home`

3. Which of the following commands creates a file of zero length?

    a. `cat >> ` *filename*

    b. `touch ` *filename*

    c. `ls -c ` *filename*

    d. `md ` *filename*

4. You can't have files called `abc` and `ABC` in the same directory. True or False?

5. Which of the following commands removes a file called `-l`?

    a. `rm -l`

    b. `rm --ignore -l`

    c. `rm -- -l`

    d. `rm --`

LINUX FILE SYSTEM MANAGEMENT

Labs included in this chapter

- Lab 4.1 Exploring the Filesystem Hierarchy Standard
- Lab 4.2 Working with BASH Aliases
- Lab 4.3 Using Advanced `find` Options
- Lab 4.4 Working with File and Directory Permissions
- Lab 4.5 Using the Advanced Features of `slocate`

CompTIA Linux+ Exam Objectives

Objective		Lab
103.1	Work on the command line	4.2–4.5
103.3	Perform basic file management	4.3–4.5
104.7	Find system files and place files in the correct location	4.1, 4.4, 4.5
105.1	Customize and use the shell environment	4.2

Lab 4.1 Exploring the Filesystem Hierarchy Standard

Objectives

The goal of this lab is to learn about the Filesystem Hierarchy Standard (FHS) by exploring the FHS Web site. When you understand FHS, you know where files should be placed in the file system.

Materials Required

This lab requires the following:

- A computer running Fedora 13 Linux

Estimated completion time: 30 minutes

Activity

1. Log in to your Linux computer as an ordinary user.

2. Start a Web browser, and go to **www.pathname.com/fhs/**.

3. Click **FHS 2.3 HTML**, and then examine the Table of Contents.

4. Click **The Filesystem** and read the section "Chapter 2. The Filesystem." It explains that the FHS applies to any file system supporting the same basic security features found in most UNIX file systems. These file systems include Linux but not non-UNIX operating systems, such as Windows. You also learn that files are placed in four categories: shareable, unshareable, variable, and static. Press **PageUp** or **Home** to return to the Table of Contents.

5. Click **Purpose** under the heading "The Root Filesystem." Note the caution that "Applications must never create or require special files or subdirectories in the root directory" and the reasons for this caution. Users shouldn't do this, either, but if permissions are set up correctly, the only user capable of doing so is the root user.

6. Go back to the Table of Contents. Click the **/bin : Essential user command binaries (for use by all users)** link, and read the "Purpose" section. The /bin directory is required so that the system can run and be administered at a basic level, even when no other file systems are mounted. This section also tells you the files that must be in this directory.

7. Go back to the Table of Contents. Click **/etc : Host-specific system configuration**, and read the "Purpose" and "Requirements" sections. The /etc directory and any subdirectories contain files for configuring the system, daemons, and applications. No executable programs (binaries) can be stored in this directory structure, according to the FHS.

8. Read the "Specific Options" section, which states that certain subdirectories must exist but only "if the corresponding subsystem is installed." The best example is the X11 subdirectory, which must exist only if you're running the X Window system (the graphics system). If your Linux computer is running as a server and has no graphical system installed, the X11 subdirectory isn't needed. Some Linux distributions install it anyway.

9. Go back to the Table of Contents. Click **/home : User home directories (optional)**, and read the "Purpose" and "Requirements" sections. The word "optional" means the /home directory isn't required for a system to be FHS compatible. An administrator can devise a different method for handling users' home directories.

NOTE Users' home directories don't have to be in the /home directory. You can put them in any FHS-compliant place, such as /var/home . If you do, however, you have to modify the home directory's location in the /etc/passwd file.

10. Go back to the Table of Contents. Click **/lib : Essential shared libraries and kernel modules,** and read the "Purpose" and "Specific Options" sections. Notice that there's usually a `modules` subdirectory of /lib because most Linux distributions use kernel modules.

11. Go back to the Table of Contents. Click **/lib<qual> : Alternate format essential shared libraries (optional),** and read the entire section. In the future, you're likely to run a 64-bit version of Linux. When you do, you'll probably have the directories mentioned in this section: /lib32, /lib64, and a /lib symbolic link to one of them.

12. Go back to the Table of Contents. Click **/sbin : System binaries,** and read the entire section. Pay attention to the footnotes, which state that "Programs executed after /usr is known to be mounted (when there are no problems) are generally placed in /usr/sbin. Locally installed system administration programs should be placed in /usr/local/sbin." Follow this guideline when you're installing additional system administration software.

13. Go back to the Table of Contents. Click **/tmp : Temporary files,** and read the entire section. The most important concept is that any files placed in this directory aren't expected to survive a system shutdown and startup. How this issue is handled is a local matter, however. Some Linux distributions erase all files in the /tmp directory on startup, and some don't.

14. Exit the Web browser and stay logged in if you're continuing to the next lab; otherwise, shut down the computer.

TIP If you have time, you can do more FHS-related reading and explore links to information on the /usr and /var directory structures.

Review Questions

1. The FHS specifies which of the following categories of files? (Choose all that apply.)
   a. Shareable versus unshareable
   b. Variable versus static
   c. Read-only versus read-write
   d. Those having owners versus those with no owners

2. Which directory is used for storing variable data files?
   a. /etc
   b. /var
   c. /usr
   d. /home

3. Which directory is used for storing static configuration files?

    a.   `/etc`

    b.   `/var`

    c.   `/usr`

    d.   `/home`

4. Creating new directories in the root of the file system is allowed. True or False?

5. Which directory is used for storing shared library images?

    a.   `/etc`

    b.   `/var`

    c.   `/usr`

    d.   `/lib`

Lab 4.2 Working with BASH Aliases

Objectives

The goal of this lab is to become familiar with BASH aliases. You learn how to display, add, delete, and redefine aliases.

Materials Required

This lab requires the following:

- A computer running Fedora 13 Linux

Estimated completion time: 20 minutes

Activity Background

Many Linux commands are affected by aliases that have been defined. For example, you learned in Chapter 4 that when you use the `mv` command, you're actually running `mv -i` because an alias has been defined to change `mv` to `mv -i`. In this lab, you create BASH aliases that are in effect while you're logged in and are removed after you log out. If you want them to be permanent, you must add them to a startup script. With Fedora, you can add them to the .bashrc file in your home directory.

Activity

1. Switch to a command-line terminal (`tty2`) by pressing **Ctrl+Alt+F2**, and log in to the terminal as any user.

2. To display existing aliases, type **alias** and press **Enter**. You see output similar to the following:

```
alias cp='cp-i'
alias l.='ls -d .* --color=auto'
alias ll='ls -l --color=auto'
alias ls='ls --color=auto'
alias mv='mv -i'
```

```
alias rm='rm -i'
alias which='alias | /usr/bin/which --tty-only --read-alias
    --show-dot --show-tilde''
```

3. Add an alias by typing **alias lspasswd="less /etc/passwd"** and pressing **Enter**.

4. To see the alias you've added to the BASH shell, type **alias** and press **Enter**.

5. To try your new alias, type **lspasswd** and press **Enter**. The contents of the /etc/passwd file are displayed onscreen. Because this file is being displayed by the less command, press **q** to go back to the shell prompt.

6. Suppose you want to return to the shell prompt immediately after the file is displayed instead of having to press q. There's no easy way to edit an alias, so you have to just replace the old alias with a new alias. Type **alias lspasswd="cat /etc/passwd"** and press **Enter**.

7. To verify that the alias has changed, type **alias** and press **Enter**, and then type **lspasswd** and press **Enter**.

8. To delete the lspasswd alias, type **unalias lspasswd** and press **Enter**. Verify that it's deleted by entering the **alias** command again.

9. Next, you create an alias to shut the system down, but you use the -k option so that the system doesn't actually shut down. Type **alias goodnight="shutdown -h now -k"** and press **Enter**.

10. Type **goodnight** and press **Enter**. Notice that the shutdown message is displayed.

11. To prevent the shell from running an alias, you can precede a command with the shell's escape character—usually a backslash. Type **\goodnight** at the shell prompt and press **Enter**. You see the message "Command not found" because the shell didn't treat goodnight as an alias. Instead, it looked for a command named goodnight to run but didn't find it.

12. You can have more than one alias on a command line. When the first alias ends in a space, the shell tries to expand the next word on the command line. Create two aliases by typing the following, pressing **Enter** after each line. Make sure you add the space before the closing quote in the first line:

```
alias a="echo "
alias b="Hello World"
```

13. When you enter both aliases on the command line, they combine to perform the command echo Hello World. Type **a b** (making sure you have a space between a and b) and press **Enter**. You see the following result:

```
Hello World
```

14. To see how the shell tries to expand aliases recursively, create these three aliases:

```
alias 1="ls -l"
alias 2="1"
alias 3="2"
```

Type **3** and press **Enter** to display a directory listing in the long format. The shell expanded the 3 into 2, then the 2 into 1, and finally the 1 into ls -l.

15. To see the problems that can happen if you define a common command as something else, type **alias cd="shutdown -h now -k"** and press **Enter**, and then type **cd /etc** and press **Enter**. The system carries out the shutdown command instead of the cd command and displays /etc because it assumes /etc is the message argument to the shutdown command.

4

16. To delete the aliases you have created, log out by typing **logout** and pressing **Enter**. Log in again, and then type **alias** and press **Enter** to verify that your aliases have been deleted. Stay logged in if you're continuing to the next lab.

Review Questions

1. Which command displays all existing aliases?

   a. `lsalias`

   b. `ls --alias`

   c. `alias`

   d. `alias --show`

2. Which command creates the zz alias?

   a. `alias zz="ls -al"`

   b. `mkalias zz "ls -al"`

   c. `alias -c ls -al`

   d. `unalias zz`

3. Which command deletes the zz alias?

   a. `alias -d zz`

   b. `delalias zz`

   c. `alias --del zz`

   d. `unalias zz`

4. You can prevent the shell from expanding an alias by doing which of the following?

   a. Compiling the shell with the `--noexpand` option

   b. Preceding the alias with a backslash

   c. Using uppercase characters for the alias name

   d. Preceding the alias with a period

5. If you want to modify an alias named xx, you use the `alias -e zz` command. True or False?

Lab 4.3 Using Advanced `find` Options

Objectives

The goal of this lab is to learn how to use the `find` command's advanced options. These options are useful for system administrators who must manage computers' file systems.

Materials Required

This lab requires the following:

- A computer running Fedora 13 Linux

Estimated completion time: 20 minutes

Activity

1. Switch to a command-line terminal (`tty2`) by pressing **Ctrl+Alt+F2**, and log in to the terminal as the root user.

2. A common administration problem is dealing with files and directories with owners who don't exist. This problem happens when users are removed from the system, but their files aren't removed. You can use the `-nouser` option to display a list of these files and directories. Type **find / -nouser** and press **Enter**.

3. If you're using a fresh Fedora installation, you probably don't have any files with owners who don't exist, but you can use the `chown` command to assign an invalid owner to a file. Type **touch test** and press **Enter** create a file in the current directory. Next, type **chown 7000 test** and press **Enter** to assign a nonexistent user as the file owner. Repeat Step 2, and you should see `/root/test` displayed.

4. You can also use the chown command to fix any files that aren't owned by a valid user. Type **chown nobody test** and press **Enter**. The user `nobody` (a user created automatically by Linux) is now the file owner. Repeat Step 2, and notice that the file isn't listed.

When you do these steps, you might see a message similar to "find: /proc/1710/fd/4: No such file or directory." This message is normal, so it isn't shown in the steps.

5. An administrator might want to know which files on the system are set to the SUID permission. You can use the `-perm` option to list these files, but you need to specify the SUID permission correctly. For example, to use numeric representation for this permission (4000), type **find / -perm +4000** and press **Enter**.

6. You can use the `-size` option to display all files larger than a specified value. For large files, you must specify kilobytes because there's no way to specify megabytes. For example, to list all files on your system larger than 256 KB, type **find / -size 256k** and press **Enter**.

7. Until now, you've been searching the entire file system, but you can search a smaller portion of it by specifying a directory. For example, to list the symbolic links in the `/sbin` directory, type **find /sbin -type l** and press **Enter**.

8. Another good use of the `find` command is locating files that have been accessed or modified in a certain time period. For example, to list files in the `/etc` directory that have been accessed in the past 60 minutes, type **find /etc -amin -60** and press **Enter**. To see a list of files that have been modified in the past day, type **find /etc -mtime -1** and press **Enter**.

The `-amin` argument looks for files that have been accessed in a specified number of minutes. You can also use `-mmin` to look for files that have been modified. The `-mtime` and `-atime` arguments look for files that have been modified or accessed in a specified number of days.

So far, you've focused on displaying files and directories that match a criterion, but you can use `find` to perform other actions when files match criteria. In Steps 2 and 3, you used `find` to locate files with no user owners. In Step 4, you used `chown` to assign owners to these files. You can combine these two steps into one. For example, the following command changes the group owner to the `users` group for all files and directories with no group owner:

```
find / -nogroup -exec chgrp users "{}" ";"
```

 The `exec` parameter specifies running the `chgrp` command every time `find` locates a file with no owner. The braces ({ }) are a placeholder for the name of the unowned file, and the semicolon (;) signals the end of the command.

9. The `find` command has many more options. To get help with this command, type **man find** and press **Enter**. Browse through the man pages, and when you're finished, press **q** to quit. Type **logout** and press **Enter**, and then press **Ctrl+Alt+F1** to go back to the graphical screen.

Review Questions

1. Which of the following displays a list of files in the current directory that have no valid user owners?

    a. `find /bin -nogroup`

    b. `find . -nouser`

    c. `find / user=""`

    d. `find nouser`

2. Which command finds files in the `/bin` directory that have been modified in the past hour?

    a. `find /bin -amin -60`

    b. `find -bin /amin -1`

    c. `find /bin -mmin -60`

    d. `find /bin -mtime -1`

3. Which of the following produces a list of all files on your hard disk set to the SUID permission?

    a. `find / -perm +1000`

    b. `find / -perm +2000`

    c. `find / -perm +4000`

    d. `find / -perm +777`

4. Which command produces a list of files that are equal to or greater than 2 MB?

    a. `find / -size gt 2MB`

    b. `find / -size => 2000000`

    c. `find / -size 2048k`

    d. `find / -size 2M`

5. Which command produces a list of all symbolic links on your hard disk?

    a. `find / -type l`

    b. `find / -symlinks`

    c. `find / -type s`

    d. `find / -links`

Lab 4.4 Working with File and Directory Permissions

Objectives

The goal of this lab is to understand how to work with the details of file and directory permissions. In particular, you see how the sticky bit operates as a special permissions function.

Materials Required

This lab requires the following:

- A computer running Fedora 13 Linux

Estimated completion time: 20 minutes

Activity Background

In this lab, you're logged in as three users simultaneously: the root user and two ordinary users. You create files as one ordinary user and see the effects on the other ordinary user. You're also logged in as root so that you can perform tasks ordinary users can't do.

Activity

1. Switch to a command-line terminal (`tty2`) by pressing **Ctrl+Alt+F2**, and log in to the terminal as the root user.

2. Create a directory by typing **mkdir /var/local/share** and pressing **Enter**.

3. Type **ls -ld /var/local/share** and press **Enter**. Check the output to make sure the `share` directory has these permissions:

   ```
   drwxr-xr-x 2 root root 4096 Aug 18 15:23 /var/local/share
   ```

If you use the command `ls -l /var/local/share` (omitting the d option), you see a list of the directory's contents instead of the directory. Of course, the directory is empty because you just created it.

If the permissions are different, type **chmod 755 /var/local/share** and press **Enter**.

4. This lab requires two ordinary user accounts. You should already have one set up; for this lab, assume it's called matt. If you don't have a second account, you need to create one named beth. (If your first user is named beth, choose another name.) Add a new user by typing **useradd beth** and pressing **Enter**. Next, type **passwd beth** and press **Enter**, and then enter a password you can remember easily.

5. Switch to virtual console 3 by pressing **Ctrl+Alt+F3**. Log in as beth. Type **cd /var/local/share** and press **Enter**.

6. Switch to virtual console 4 by pressing **Ctrl+Alt+F4**. Log in as matt. Type **cd /var/local/share** and press **Enter**.

7. Try to create a file by typing **echo "Hello from Matt" > file1** and pressing **Enter**. You see the following error message because you don't have write permission to the share directory:

```
-bash: file1: Permission denied
```

8. Switch to virtual console 2 by pressing **Ctrl+Alt+F2**. You're logged in as root. To give all users write permission to the share directory, type **chmod o+w /var/local/share** and press **Enter**.

9. Switch to virtual console 4 by pressing **Ctrl+Alt+F4**. You're logged in as matt. Again, try to create a file by typing **echo "Hello from Matt" > file1** and pressing **Enter**. (*Tip*: Instead of retyping this command, you can recall it by using the up arrow.) This time it should succeed, and no error message is displayed.

10. Type **ls -l file1** and press **Enter**. Notice the file permissions, and note that matt is the user and group owner:

```
-rw-rw-r--. 1 matt matt 16 Aug 18 15:23 file1
```

11. Switch to virtual console 3 by pressing **Ctrl+Alt+F3**. You're logged in as beth. Type **ls -l** and press **Enter**, and notice that you get the same result as in Step 10.

12. Type **cat file1** and press **Enter**. You see the contents of the file displayed because beth has read permission to matt's file:

```
Hello from Matt
```

13. Try to append (write) to the file by typing **echo "Hello from Beth" >> file1** and pressing **Enter**. This command fails, and you see an error message because beth doesn't have write permission to matt's file.

The >> operator specifies appending to a file instead of overwriting it.

14. Switch to virtual console 2 by pressing **Ctrl+Alt+F2**. You're logged in as the root user. Enter **cd /var/local/share** and press **Enter** to change to the share directory. Try to append (write) to the file by typing **echo "Hello from root" >> file1** and pressing **Enter**. This command succeeds because the root user has access to all files and directories on the system, regardless of permissions.

15. Switch to virtual console 3 by pressing **Ctrl+Alt+F3**. You're logged in as beth. Type **cat file1** and press **Enter**, and you see the following:

```
Hello from Matt
Hello from root
```

16. Type **rm file1** and press **Enter**. If you're asked whether you want to remove the file, type **y**. Type **ls -l** and press **Enter**. Notice that the file no longer exists because beth was able to erase matt's file. You might think that because she has only read access to the file, she shouldn't be able to erase it. However, beth has write access to the /var/local/share

directory, which enables her to delete matt's files. You can solve this security problem by setting the sticky bit on the directory, as shown in the next step.

17. Switch to virtual console 2 by pressing **Ctrl+Alt+F2**. You're logged in as the root user. Type **chmod o+t /var/local/share** and press **Enter**. Next, type **ls -ld /var/local/share** and press **Enter**. As shown in the following line, the sticky bit (t) has been added in place of the x bit:

```
drwxr-xrwt 2 root root 4096 Aug 18 15:23 /var/local/share
```

You'll probably also see that /var/local/share is highlighted in green to indicate that the sticky bit is set.

18. Switch to virtual console 4 by pressing **Ctrl+Alt+F4**. You're logged in as matt. Create file1 by using the same command as in Step 9. Verify that the file was created by typing **ls -l** and pressing **Enter**.

19. Switch to virtual console 3 by pressing **Ctrl+Alt+F3**. You're logged in as beth. Again, try to delete the file by typing **rm file1** and pressing **Enter**. You're prompted with this line: rm: remove write-protected regular file 'file1'?.

20. Type **y** and press **Enter**. You see the following error message stating that you can't erase the file:

```
rm: cannot remove 'file1': Operation not permitted
```

21. Log out of each terminal session, and press **Ctrl+Alt+F1** to go back to the graphical screen.

Review Questions

1. Which command appends data to a file?

   a. `echo "November 5, 2013" > /tmp/audit`

   b. `find / -nouser >> /tmp/audit`

   c. `ls -l | /tmp/audit`

   d. `cat /tmp/audit`

2. Which command saves data to a file by overwriting existing data in the file?

   a. `echo "November 5, 2013" > /tmp/audit`

   b. `find / -nouser >> /tmp/audit`

   c. `ls -l | /tmp/audit`

   d. `cat /tmp/audit`

3. Which command gives all users write access to the bboard directory?

   a. `chmod 754 bboard`

   b. `chmod 777 bboard`

   c. `chmod 1754 bboard`

   d. `chmod 4754 bboard`

4. If users have write access to a directory but the sticky bit permission isn't set, any user can erase any file in the directory, regardless of ownership. True or False?

5. You want to set the sticky bit permission for the `elvis` directory. Which of the following commands should you use? (Choose all that apply.)

   a. `chmod 4000 elvis`

   b. `chmod 1000 elvis`

   c. `chmod o+t elvis`

   d. `chmod o+s elvis`

Lab 4.5 Using the Advanced Features of `slocate`

Objectives

The goal of this lab is to learn the features of the `slocate` command, which is an advanced version of the GNU `locate` command with additional security features. With `slocate`, users can't see files in the file system if they don't have permissions to them.

Materials Required

This lab requires the following:

* A computer running Fedora 13 Linux

Estimated completion time: 30 minutes

Activity

1. Switch to a command-line terminal (`tty2`) by pressing **Ctrl+Alt+F2**, and log in to the terminal as the root user.

2. Go to your home directory typing **cd ~** (or just **cd**) and pressing **Enter**.

3. To check whether you have a `test` subdirectory, type **ls test** and press **Enter**. This subdirectory should exist from a previous lab, but if it doesn't, create it with the **mkdir test** command.

4. Create a file in this subdirectory by typing **echo "Hello World" > test/sample99** and pressing **Enter**.

5. To see whether `locate` can find this file, type **locate sample99** and press **Enter**. Unless you happen to have a file with this name in another directory, `locate` doesn't find it because you just created it, and your computer updates the `mlocate.db` database file only once a day.

6. To force your computer to update its database now, type **updatedb** and press **Enter**. This command might take a while to run because it's scanning nearly all the hard disk. To reduce the time the update takes, you can exclude directories from the scan with the `-e` option. Here's an example of excluding most directories from the scan except `/root` and `/home`:

   ```
   updatedb -e "/tmp,/etc,/usr,/var,/bin,/sbin,/boot"
   ```

7. The `updatedb` command uses the `/etc/updatedb.conf` configuration file. Display this file's contents by using a command you have learned (such as `cat`, `less`, or `more`). You should see output similar to the following:

```
PRUNE_BIND_MOUNTS = "yes"
PRUNEFS = "9p afs anon_inodefs auto autofs bdev"
```

8. The `PRUNEFS` line specifies file systems that `updatedb` doesn't scan, and the `PRUNEPATHS` line specifies directories that `updatedb` doesn't scan. You can specify other directories to exclude by editing the `/etc/updatedb.conf` file or using the `-e` option in the `updatedb` command, as explained in Step 6. Type **locate sample99** and press **Enter**. The `sample99` file should be listed.

9. Log in as an ordinary user with the **su** command. For example, if your user account name is joe, type **su joe** and press **Enter**.

10. Try to find the `sample99` file by typing **locate sample99** and pressing **Enter**. The file shouldn't be found because you're logged in as an ordinary user, and `sample99` is in a directory you don't have permission to access.

11. Fedora and many other Linux distributions use the more secure `slocate` command instead of `locate`. To see this, type **ls -l /usr/bin/locate** and press **Enter**. As the following line shows, `locate` is actually a symbolic link to the `slocate` command. (The `/usr/bin/locate` part should be highlighted in orange to indicate a symbolic link.)

```
lrwxrwxrwx 1 root slocate 7 Mar 28 15:55 /usr/bin/locate
```

Go back to the shell you were using when logged in as root by typing **exit** and pressing **Enter**.

12. Give other users temporary access to the `/root` directory by typing **chmod -R 755 /root** and pressing **Enter**. The current permissions to `/root` are set to 750; by setting them to 755, you have given all other users read and execute permissions, which are required to find files with `locate`.

13. Update the `update` database by typing **updatedb** and pressing **Enter**.

14. Log in as an ordinary user with the **su** command. Try to find the `sample99` file again by typing **locate sample99** and pressing **Enter**. You should find the file because your user account now has access to the `/root/test` directory.

15. Go back to the shell you were using when logged in as root by using the **exit** command. Restore the `/root` directory so that other users no longer have access to it by typing **chmod -R 750 /root** and pressing **Enter**.

16. Log out. Press **Ctrl+Alt+F1** to go back to the graphical screen, and shut down the computer unless you're going on to the next chapter.

Review Questions

1. How often is the `mlocate.db` database updated?

   a. Hourly

   b. Daily

   c. Monthly

   d. As soon as files have changed

2. What command do you use to force the `mlocate.db` database to update immediately?

3. When updating the database, almost all directories on the hard disk are scanned, which can take a long time. Which of the following commands do you use to prevent the `/var` directory from being scanned?

   a.   `locatedb -f "/var"`

   b.   `updatedb --novar`

   c.   `updatedb -e "/var"`

   d.   `locatedb | grep "/var"`

4. You can exclude the `/home` directory from the database scan by adding it to the `PRUNEPATHS` line in the `/etc/updatedb.conf` file. True or False?

5. For an ordinary user to find a file with `locate`, it must be in a directory the user has permission to access, which means the directory must have only the execute (x) permission set. True or False?

LINUX FILE SYSTEM ADMINISTRATION

Labs included in this chapter

- Lab 5.1 Mounting and Ejecting DVDs/CDs
- Lab 5.2 Working with USB Memory
- Lab 5.3 Using the `fuser` Command

CompTIA Linux+ Exam Objectives

Objective		Lab
103.1	Work at the command line	5.2, 5.3
103.5	Create, monitor, and kill processes	5.3
104.3	Control mounting and unmounting of file systems	5.1, 5.2

Lab 5.1 Mounting and Ejecting DVDs/CDs

Objectives

The goal of this lab is to become familiar with automounting. You experiment with mounting, unmounting, and ejecting DVDs/CDs. You also learn that you can't unmount a DVD/CD if the mount point is in your current directory. Most Linux distributions use `autofs` for automounting.

Materials Required

This lab requires the following:

- A computer with a DVD/CD drive running Fedora 13 Linux
- A CD or DVD containing information, such as the Fedora 13 Linux installation disc

Estimated completion time: 10 minutes

Activity Background

You should begin this lab without a DVD/CD in the drive.

Most desktop computers have DVD/CD drives with trays that can be controlled by software. That is, the software opens and closes the tray. Most notebook computers have DVD/CD trays that software can open but not close. If you're using a notebook computer for this lab, some steps might not work as written.

Activity

1. Start your Fedora 13 Linux system and log in to the GUI.

2. Open the DVD/CD tray by pressing the button on the drive's front panel. Insert a data DVD/CD, such as the Linux installation disc.

3. Close the tray by pressing the **eject** button on the front panel. If you're using a notebook computer, push the tray closed manually. Wait a few seconds. File Browser should open and list the files on the DVD/CD.

4. Open a terminal window by clicking **Applications,** pointing to **System Tools,** and clicking **Terminal.**

5. View the mounted disc's details by typing **mount** and pressing **Enter.** The last line of output from the `mount` command should be similar to `/dev/sr0 on /media/VolumeName type udf ...` (with *VolumeName* representing the DVD/CD drive's name).

6. Open the drive tray by typing **eject** and pressing **Enter.**

7. To check whether the DVD/CD is mounted, type **mount** and press **Enter.** You shouldn't see the line of output that was displayed in Step 5 because the DVD/CD was unmounted before it was ejected.

8. Close the drive tray by typing **eject -t** and pressing **Enter.**

9. Wait a few seconds, and then check whether the DVD/CD is mounted by typing **mount** and pressing **Enter**. A File Browser window should open, and you should see the same line of output you saw in Step 5.

10. To make your current directory the mount point directory for the DVD/CD, type **cd /media/*VolumeName*** (replacing *VolumeName* with the name of the volume you saw in the mount command's output) and press **Enter**.

11. Type **eject** and press **Enter**. You should see an error message similar to "umount: /media/VolumeName: device is busy" along with some additional information. The DVD/CD won't eject because you're in the directory in which it's mounted.

12. Another way to unmount a device is to use the `umount` command. Type **umount /media/*VolumeName*** and press **Enter**. You should see the error message "Unmount failed: Cannot unmount because file system on device is busy."

13. Move out of the mount point directory by typing **cd** and pressing **Enter**. Type **umount /media/*VolumeName*** and press **Enter** (or press the **up arrow** key twice to recall the command you used in Step 12). Type **eject** and press **Enter** to open the drive tray, and remove the DVD/CD from the drive.

14. Close the terminal window by typing **exit** and pressing **Enter** or by clicking the × in the upper-right corner. If you're going on to the next lab, leave your system running; otherwise, shut down the system.

If you're in the mount point directory, you might be able to use the eject button on the DVD/CD drive. If you do, you won't be able to mount to the DVD/CD drive again until you move out of the mount point directory.

Review Questions

1. In what path was your DVD/CD mounted?

2. If you see the message "umount: /media/*VolumeName*: device is busy" when you try to unmount a DVD/CD, what's wrong?

   a. There's no DVD/CD in the drive tray.

   b. You're in the current mount point directory.

   c. The DVD/CD drive tray is open.

   d. The DVD/CD device drivers need to be updated.

3. Which command closes the drive tray?

   a. `eject`

   b. `eject -a on`

   c. `eject -t`

   d. `eject /dev/cdrom`

4. The umount command always works, even if the eject command fails to unmount the DVD/CD and open the drive tray. True or False?

5. Write the command to unmount a DVD/CD volume named Fedora13Inst without opening the drive tray.

Lab 5.2 Working with USB Memory

Objectives

The goal of this lab is to become familiar with USB memory devices, called thumb drives, flash drives, and other terms.

Materials Required

This lab requires the following:

- A computer with a free USB port running Fedora 13 Linux
- A USB flash drive

Estimated completion time: 20 minutes

Activity

1. Switch to a command-line terminal (tty2) by pressing **Ctrl+Alt+F2**, and log in to the terminal as the root user.

2. Monitor the messages log file by typing **tail -f /var/log/messages** and pressing **Enter**. You can ignore any messages displayed onscreen.

3. Connect a USB memory device to your computer by plugging it into a USB port. You should see the contents of the messages log file displayed, as shown:

   ```
   fedora13 kernel: Initializing USB Mass Storage driver...
   fedora13 kernel: sd 3:0:0:0: [sdb] Attached SCSI removable disk
   ```

   In particular, look for a line similar to the second line. The most important information is [sdb], which tells you that the system sees the USB memory device as the sdb device —a SCSI drive. If you see something different, such as sda or sdc, modify subsequent steps in this lab accordingly.

4. Press **Ctrl+C** to get back to the command prompt. To create a mount point for the USB memory device, type **mkdir /mnt/usb** and press **Enter**.

5. Mount the device to the mount point you just created by typing **mount -t vfat /dev/sdb1 /mnt/usb** and pressing **Enter**. Remember to replace sdb in this command with what you saw in the messages file in Step 3, if necessary. The -t vfat parameter is used with USB drives formatted as FAT32. If yours is formatted as FAT, use -t msdos instead.

6. Make the mount point directory your current directory by typing **cd /mnt/usb** and pressing **Enter**.

7. Use the ls command to view the flash drive's contents.

8. Create a new file by typing **touch newfile** and pressing **Enter**. Use the ls command again to verify that the file has been created.

9. Type **mount** and press **Enter** to see how the USB memory device is mounted. You should see a line similar to the following at the end of the output:

```
/dev/sdb1 on /mnt/usb type vfat (rw)
```

This output tells you that the device is formatted with the VFAT file system (FAT32) and is mounted for read and write access (`rw`).

When you buy a USB memory device, it's formatted with a FAT file system so that Windows users can use it. You can reformat the device with a Linux file system.

10. Type **fdisk -l /dev/sdb** and press **Enter**. You see output similar to the following:

```
Device    Boot  Start    End      Blocks    Id   System
/dev/sdb1        8      28642     15634496   c    W95  FAT32 (LBA)
```

This output indicates that the device looks like a hard disk to Linux because it has a partition table. It uses the first partition (`sdb1`).

5

11. USB memory devices require the support of the USB storage kernel module. To confirm that this module is installed, type **lsmod | more** and press **Enter**. Near the top of the output, you see a line similar to this:

```
usb_storage  34392  1
```

12. Press **q** to return to the command prompt. Unplug the USB memory device from the computer. Type **ls** and press **Enter** to display the contents of the USB memory device again. You might still see the directory listing of the drive's contents because Linux cached the information. After a short while, the cache expires, and there's no output from the `ls` command.

13. Type **mount** and press **Enter**. The output `/dev/sdb1 on /mnt/usb type vfat (rw)` means Linux thinks the device is still mounted.

14. Type **tail -f /var/log/messages** and press **Enter**. Plug the device back into the same USB port and note the output that's displayed. You should see a line similar to `sdc: sdc1`, which tells you that Linux thinks your USB memory device is a different device (`sdc`).

15. Press **Ctrl+C** to exit the `tail` command. Type **cd** and press **Enter** to leave the mount point. Type **umount /mnt/usb** and press **Enter**.

16. Unplug the flash drive. If you're going on to the next lab, leave your system running; otherwise, shut down the system.

Review Questions

1. What does the `tail` command do?

2. USB memory devices are displayed in Linux as which of the following?

   a. 3.5-inch disk drives

   b. Normal IDE hard disks

   c. SCSI hard disks

   d. Zip drives

3. USB memory devices require the support of what kernel module?

4. With the `mount` command, how do you specify that a device uses the FAT32 file system?

    a.   `-t fat32`

    b.   `-t msdos`

    c.   `-t vfat`

    d.   `-t win95`

5. When you plug in a USB memory device, Linux automounts it. True or False?

Lab 5.3 Using the `fuser` Command

Objectives

The goal of this lab is to become familiar with the `fuser` command, which enables you to see which users or daemons are holding files open. You might need to know this information if you want to perform an operation on a file but some other user has it open. Also, when you're writing a program, this information can tell you when it has an error.

Materials Required

This lab requires the following:

- A computer running Fedora 13 Linux

Estimated completion time: 15 minutes

Activity

1. If necessary, switch to a command-line terminal (`tty2`) by pressing **Ctrl+Alt+F2**, and log in to the terminal as the root user.

2. Switch to virtual console 3 by pressing **Ctrl+Alt+F3**, and then log in as the root user.

3. Create a zero-length file by typing **touch sample** and pressing **Enter**.

4. Open the file and hold it open by typing **less sample** and pressing **Enter**.

5. Switch to virtual console 2 by pressing **Ctrl+Alt+F2**.

6. You can use `fuser` to find the process that's holding the `sample` file open. First, type **fuser *** and press **Enter** to see all open files in the current directory. To see which process is holding the `sample` file open, type **fuser sample** and press **Enter**. You should see output similar to the following:

```
sample: 2650
```

This output tells you that process 2650 is holding the file open. Your process number will probably be different.

7. See what process 2650 is by typing **ps XX** (replacing *XX* with your process number) and pressing **Enter**. You should see output similar to the following:

```
PID    TTY    STAT    TIME    COMMAND
2650   tty3   S       0:00    less sample
```

This output tells you that process 2650 was started from virtual console 3 (`tty3`).

8. To find out who's logged in on `tty3`, **type w | grep tty3** and press **Enter**. You should see output similar to the following:

```
root  tty3  -  23:47  1:14m  0.60s  0.60s less sample
```

The `w` command shows you who's logged in to a computer and what program he or she is running. Similar commands are `who` and `whoami`.

9. Steps 1 through 8 show how to identify a process that has a file open and determine the user running the process. You can also use `fuser` to troubleshoot system problems. Type **fuser /var/log/*** and press **Enter**. You should see output similar to this:

```
/var/log/cron:      57
/var/log/boot.log: 57
/var/log/maillog:  57
```

10. This output shows you that process 57 has three log files open. Type **ps XX** (replacing *XX* with the process number `fuser` returned in Step 9) and press **Enter** to find out what the process is. You should see output similar to the following:

```
PID   TTY   STAT   TIME   COMMAND
57    ?     S1     0:00   /sbin/rsyslogd -c 4
```

It's no surprise to discover that the system-logging daemon (`rsyslogd`) is holding the log files open.

11. If you're interested only in which user is holding the files open, you can use the `-u` option. Type **fuser -u /var/log/*** and press **Enter**. You should see that the root user has these files open:

```
/var/log/cron:       57(root)
/var/log/debug:      57(root)
/var/log/maillog:   57(root)
```

12. For advanced users and programmers, a particularly helpful use of `fuser` is to see what processes are using a shared library. Type **cd /lib** and press **Enter**, and then type **fuser -v *** and press **Enter**. You should see output similar to the following:

```
            USER   PID   ACCESS   COMMAND
ld-2.3.3.so root   1     ....m    init
            root   2497  ....m    Syslogd
            root   2501  ....m    klogd
            root   2529  ....m    portmap
            root   2549  ....m    rpc.statd
            root   2577  ....m    rpc.idmapd
            root   2671  ....m    smartd
            root   2681  ....m    acpid
```

The letter m after a process number means the library file is a shared library.

13. Press **Ctrl+Alt+F3** to switch to `tty3`, and press **q** to exit `less`. Type **logout** and press **Enter**. Press **Ctrl+Alt+F2** to switch back to `tty2`, and shut down the system.

5

Review Questions

1. Which command is used to hold open a very short or zero-length file?

    a. cat

    b. more

    c. less

    d. tail

2. Which command enables you to create a zero-length file?

3. Which command do you use to find the process that's holding a file open?

    a. w

    b. ps

    c. top

    d. fuser

4. Which of the following commands shows you all open files in a directory?

    a. fuser sample

    b. fuser -u sample

    c. fuser -u /proc/*

    d. fuser /var/log/messages

5. What does it mean when the letter m follows a process number in fuser output?

CHAPTER 6

ADVANCED INSTALLATION

Labs included in this chapter

- Lab 6.1 Installing Fedora Linux with a Live Media Edition
- Lab 6.2 Preparing for a Network Installation

CompTIA Linux+ Exam Objectives

Objective		Lab
101.1	Boot the system	6.1, 6.2

Lab 6.1 Installing Fedora Linux with a Live Media Edition

Objectives

The goal of this lab is to learn how to prepare a USB flash drive to start a Linux Fedora 13 installation.

Materials Required

This lab requires the following:

- A computer running Fedora 13 Linux
- A 1 GB or more USB flash drive
- A computer that can boot to a USB drive
- Knowledge of the keystroke for starting your computer to a boot menu
- An Internet connection

Estimated completion time: 30 minutes

Activity

1. Log in to your Linux computer as an ordinary user.

2. Start a Web browser, and go to **www.fedoraproject.org**. Click the **Download** link near the top of the page.

3. Click **Download Now** to download the installable live media for the latest version of Fedora. Save the file in your Documents directory.

4. After the download has finished, open a terminal window by clicking **Applications**, pointing to **System Tools**, and clicking **Terminal**.

5. Change to the Documents directory by typing **cd ~/Documents** and pressing **Enter**.

6. Insert the USB flash drive in a USB port on your computer. Wait a minute or so for it to automount. A File Browser window opens after the USB drive is mounted. (If the File Browser window doesn't open, the USB drive didn't automount, and you can skip the next step.)

7. Type **su** and press **Enter**, and when prompted, enter the root password. Type **umount /dev/sdb1** and press **Enter** to unmount the USB drive. You might need to replace /dev/sdb1 with the correct device name. If necessary, type **dmesg** and press **Enter** to see which device the USB drive is using.

8. Type **dd if=/home/*user*/Documents/*NameOfISOfile* of=/dev/sdb1** and press **Enter** (re-placing *user* with your login name and *NameOfISOfile* with the name of the file you saved in Step 3). This command writes the file, using a sector-by-sector copy, to your USB drive.

9. After the file has been copied, leave the USB flash drive inserted and restart your computer. As the computer starts, press the key to start to a boot menu (sometimes F12 or Delete). When you see the boot menu, highlight the **USB** option as the boot device and press **Enter**. The LinuxLive welcome window is displayed.

10. You can press Enter to boot to LinuxLive or simply wait for the system to boot automatically. Allow the system to boot automatically. After the system finishes booting, you have the options Try Fedora or Install to Hard Drive. If you want to try the latest version of Fedora, go ahead and click **Try Fedora**. When you're finished, remove the USB drive, and then shut down the system.

Review Questions

1. If you want to try Fedora Linux without actually installing it, what type of Linux distribution should you download?

    a.   64-bit version

    b.   Live media edition

    c.   Full installation DVD

    d.   Bootable installation version

2. What command do you use if you want to write an ISO file directly to a DVD, using a sector-by-sector copy?

    a.   `dd`

    b.   `cp -usesectors`

    c.   `dump`

    d.   `mv`

3. Which command helps you determine which device a USB drive is using?

    a.   `umount`

    b.   `usbdev`

    c.   `dmesg`

    d.   `showdev`

6

Lab 6.2 Preparing for a Network Installation

Objectives

The goal of this lab is to learn how to install Linux from a network location, such as an FTP server or HTTP server. You don't actually perform an installation, but you get to the step for entering the URL of the server hosting the installation image file.

Materials Required

This lab requires the following:

- A computer that can boot from a DVD
- The Fedora 13 bootable installation disc

Estimated completion time: 15 minutes

Activity

1. Insert the Fedora 13 installation DVD in the DVD drive, and boot your computer to the installation DVD. When you see the Welcome to Fedora 13! window, press **Tab**.

2. At the end of the boot options line, type **askmethod** and press **Enter**.

3. Press the arrow keys, if necessary, to highlight **English** as the language selection and press **Enter**. Press **Enter** again to accept US as the keyboard setting.

4. In the Installation Method window, press the **down** arrow to highlight the **URL** option and press **Enter**.

5. In the Configure TCP/IP window, accept the default setting to have your computer get an address from DHCP. Press **Tab** until **OK** is highlighted, and then press **Enter**.

6. In the URL Setup window, type the address of the server hosting the installation image file. If you were using an FTP server, the URL would look something like `ftp://server/ImageDirectory`. If you were using an HTTP server, the URL would be similar to `http://server/Imagedirectory`. You would also have to enter the correct folder on the FTP or HTTP server for the installation image file. After this step is completed, the installation proceeds as described in Chapter 2. Remove the Fedora 13 DVD, and shut down your computer.

Review Questions

1. On the Fedora 13 boot menu, what action do you take to perform a network installation?

   a. Select the "Install a new system or upgrade an existing system" option.

   b. Press the Tab key.

   c. Select the "Boot from local drive" option and then press the Esc key.

   d. Select the "Install from network" option.

2. What do you add to the boot options line to allow a network installation?

   a. `askmethod`

   b. `-netinstall`

   c. `chooseinstall`

   d. `-URL`

3. When choosing the installation method, what option do you select to install from an FTP or HTTP server?

   a. NFS directory

   b. Web

   c. URL

   d. Net

4. To configure your computer to communicate by using TCP/IP while performing a network install, you must use static addressing. True or False?

WORKING WITH THE BASH SHELL

Labs included in this chapter

- Lab 7.1 Using the BASH History Feature
- Lab 7.2 Customizing the BASH History Feature
- Lab 7.3 Customizing Shell Prompts
- Lab 7.4 Adding Automation to the BASH Prompt
- Lab 7.5 Setting CDPATH

CompTIA Linux+ Exam Objectives

Objective		Lab
103.1	Work on the command line	7.1–7.5
103.4	Use streams, pipes, and redirects	7.1, 7.2
105.1	Customize and use the shell environment	7.1,7.5
105.2	Customize and write simple scripts	7.4

Lab 7.1 Using the BASH History Feature

Objectives

The goal of this lab is to learn about the command history available with the BASH shell. With this feature, you don't have to retype shell commands you've entered previously. After finishing this lab, for example, you can use this feature to recall every command you entered by pressing the up arrow key, specifying numbers that represent a command's order in the history list, and searching for commands containing a certain string. You can also replace words in the most recent command as a shortcut to retyping the entire command.

Materials Required

This lab requires the following:

- A computer running Fedora 13 Linux

Estimated completion time: 15 minutes

Activity

1. Start your Linux system and log in to the GUI as an ordinary user. Switch to a command-line terminal (`tty2`) by pressing **Ctrl+Alt+F2**, and log in to the terminal as an ordinary user.

2. You can access the history of commands you've entered in the BASH shell in a few ways. The easiest way is using the up arrow key. Press the **up arrow** key now to see your most recent command displayed. Press **up arrow** again to see the next most recent command.

3. Clear the command line by pressing the **backspace** key.

4. To give BASH some commands to store in the history, type the following lines, pressing **Enter** after each line:

```
cd
ls -l /etc
ls -l
whoami
who
```

5. Next, check to see whether these commands were added to the history. To get a list of all commands that have been entered, type **history** and press **Enter**. The screen scrolls, but the commands you entered in Step 4 are displayed. Each command in the history list is numbered, like this:

```
79 cd
80 ls -l /etc
81 cd /proc
82 whoami
83 who
84 history
```

6. You can select any command by stepping back through the history with the up arrow key, but this method gets more cumbersome when the history list is long. An easier method is specifying the command's number or searching for it. To select and issue a command

by number, you enter an exclamation point (!) followed by the command's number. Type *!nn* (replacing *nn* with the number of the `ls -l /etc` command) and press **Enter**. You see a listing of the `/etc` directory.

7. Referring to a command by number requires displaying the history first to see all the numbers, and this method can be inefficient. Instead, you can search for the command you want by typing **!?etc?** and pressing **Enter**. Again, you see the listing of the `/etc` directory. BASH searched for the most recent command containing the string `etc` and then executed it.

8. Type **history** and press **Enter**. The second-to-last command is `ls -l /etc`, not `!?etc?`, because BASH saves only commands in the history, not the strings used to search for commands.

9. Type **!?wombat99?** and press **Enter**. Because the string `wombat99` isn't in your command history, BASH can't find it and displays the error message "-bash: !?wombat99?: event not found."

10. If the string you're searching for is at the start of the command, you can eliminate the question marks around the string. Type **!who** and press **Enter** to have BASH find and run the `who` command.

11. Suppose you want to issue the `whoami` command instead. You have to enter only one more keystroke because `who` is a more recent command in the history than `whoami` is. Type **!whoa** and press **Enter**.

12. The BASH history feature also allows substituting strings in the most recent command. To see how it works, type **cat /bin/bash | strings | grep shell | less** and press **Enter**. This lengthy command displays all strings in the `/bin/bash` file containing the word "shell." Because there are likely to be a lot of them, the output is piped through the `less` filter. Press **q** to exit `less`.

13. If you want to display strings containing the word "alias," you don't have to type another lengthy command. Just type **^shell^alias^** and press **Enter** to replace the word "shell" with "alias" in the most recent command and issue the `alias` command.

14. Press **Ctrl+Alt+F1** to return to the graphical screen. If you plan to continue to the next lab, stay logged in; otherwise, shut down your computer.

7

Review Questions

1. Which command displays a list of all recent commands?

 a. `ls --history`

 b. `ls --h`

 c. `history`

 d. `histfile`

2. Which command executes command number 213 in the history?

 a. `history 213`

 b. `!history 213`

 c. `!?213?`

 d. `!213`

3. Which command executes the most recent command containing the string /usr/sbin?

   a. `history "/usr/sbin"`

   b. `!hist "/usr/sbin"`

   c. `!?/usr/sbin?`

   d. `!"/usr/sbin"`

4. Which command executes the most recent command beginning with the string touch?

   a. `!touch`

   b. `!?touch?`

   c. `history "touch"`

   d. `hist ?touch?`

5. You want to issue the same command as the last one you entered, but you want to replace the word "report" with "summary." Which command should you use?

   a. `!^summary^report^`

   b. `?report?summary?`

   c. `^report^summary^`

   d. `| summary | report|`

Lab 7.2 Customizing the BASH History Feature

Objectives

The goal of this lab is to familiarize you with ways to customize the BASH command history feature.

Materials Required

This lab requires the following:

- A computer running Fedora 13 Linux

Estimated completion time: 20 minutes

Activity

1. Switch to a command-line terminal (`tty2`) by pressing **Ctrl+Alt+F2**, and if necessary, log in to the terminal as an ordinary user. Don't log in as root.

2. To remember commands in the history after a system is shut down and then restarted, Linux uses the `.bash_history` file, which is stored in your home directory. If necessary, go to your home directory by typing **cd** and pressing **Enter**.

3. Look at the last several lines in the `.bash_history` file by typing **tail .bash_history**. The last line of the file isn't `tail .bash_history`, and the previous command isn't `cd`, meaning the `.bash_history` file isn't up to date.

4. Type **history** and press **Enter**. The last line displayed is the `history` command, and the previous line is `tail .bash_history`. So the `history` command seems to be up to date, even though the `.bash_history` file is not. The reason is that the command

history is kept in system memory. In the next steps, you see when the `.bash_history` file is updated.

5. Type **echo 'This is my command'** and press **Enter.**

> When you use the `echo` command, it's best to use single quotes rather than double quotes around the string. Single quotes prevent the shell from trying to interpret special characters.
>
> **TIP**

6. Type **logout** and press **Enter.** Log in again as the same user.

7. Type **history** and press **Enter.** You see the command `echo 'This is my command'` near the end of the list.

8. Type **tail .bash_history** and press **Enter.** Again, you see the command `echo 'This is my command'` near the end of the list, which means the `.bash_history` file was updated when you logged out.

9. The `.bash_history` file can be quite large if you've used your computer a lot. Most of it scrolls quickly onscreen, but you can use the `more` or `less` commands to prevent scrolling. Type **history | less** and press **Enter.** You should see the oldest commands onscreen. Press the **spacebar** to see more of the file, and then exit `less` by pressing **q.**

10. You can use the `wc` (word count) command to see exactly how many commands are in the `.bash_history` file. To have lines instead of words counted, type **wc -l .bash_history** and press **Enter.** You see output similar to the following:

    ```
    1000 .bash_history
    ```

11. The preceding output shows that 1000 commands are stored in the history file, which is the default limit in Fedora. (This value might be different in other Linux distributions.) An environment variable called `HISTSIZE` is used to set this limit. To see the value of `HISTSIZE` on your system, type **set | grep HISTSIZE** and press **Enter.** You should see `HISTSIZE=1000` displayed.

12. If you want to change the limit to 5000 commands, you have to change the `HISTSIZE` variable in the startup script, called `.bashrc`, which is stored in your home directory. If the `HISTSIZE` variable is defined in this file, you can use any text editor to change the value. In Fedora, `HISTSIZE` is set to 1000 by default and isn't set initially in `.bashrc`. However, if you create the variable in `.bashrc`, you override the default value. To create the variable with a value of 5000 in `.bashrc` without using a text editor, type **echo 'HISTSIZE=5000' >> .bashrc** and press **Enter.** This new value is used the next time the BASH shell reads the `.bashrc` file—typically, when you log in again.

13. Type **logout** and press **Enter.** Log in again as the same user.

14. Type **set | grep HISTSIZE** and press **Enter.** You should see `HISTSIZE=5000` displayed to indicate that the `HISTSIZE` value has changed.

15. Type **history** and press **Enter** five times. Notice that each time you do this, a `history` command is added to the history. This is okay if you want the BASH history to be a faithful record of every command you type, but it's a waste of file space if you use the BASH history feature mainly as a way to save keystrokes.

16. You can configure BASH to not add a command to the history if it's the same as the previous command. To do this, you add an environment variable called `HISTCONTROL`

and assign it the value `ignoredups`. You can add it to your `.bashrc` file, similar to what you did in Step 12. Type **echo 'HISTCONTROL=ignoredups' >> .bashrc** and press **Enter**. This new value is used the next time the BASH shell reads the `.bashrc` file—usually when you log in again.

17. Log out and log back in as the same user.

18. Type **history** and press **Enter**, and repeat this step several times. Notice that even though you're entering the same command repeatedly, only one `history` command is added to the history.

19. Press **Ctrl+Alt+F1** to return to the graphical screen. If you plan to continue to the next lab, stay logged in; otherwise, shut down your computer.

Review Questions

1. In which file are commands saved in history?

   a. `.bashrc`

   b. `profile`

   c. `.bash_history`

   d. `.history`

2. The BASH history file is updated:

   a. When you log in

   b. When you log out

   c. When you issue any BASH command

   d. When the file system cache is flushed to disk

3. Which command displays how many lines are in the `.bash_history` file?

   a. `grep "*" .bash_history`

   b. `wc -l .bash_history`

   c. `ls -l .bash_history`

   d. `history --lines`

4. How many commands does BASH typically save to the history file if the `HISTSIZE` variable hasn't been added?

   a. 500

   b. 650

   c. 800

   d. 1000

5. How do you eliminate consecutive duplicate commands from being saved to the BASH history?

   a. You must recompile BASH with the `--suppressdups` switch.

   b. Set the `HISTCONTROL` environment variable's value to `ignoredups`.

   c. Hold the Ctrl key down when you type a command.

   d. Enter the command `echo "1" > /proc/sys/kernel/bash/duplicates`.

Lab 7.3 Customizing Shell Prompts

Objectives

The goal of this lab is to see how to control the most often used shell prompts: PS1 and PS2.

Materials Required

This lab requires the following:

- A computer running Fedora 13 Linux

Estimated completion time: 20 minutes

Activity

1. Switch to a command-line terminal (tty2) by pressing **Ctrl+Alt+F2**, and if necessary, log in to the terminal with any username.

2. You can configure the main BASH prompt by setting the value of the PS1 environment variable. For example, instead of displaying a static string as a prompt, you might want the string to be dynamic, such as showing the current directory or the current time. To have the BASH prompt display the current system time in 24-hour format, type **PS1='\t:'** and press **Enter**. You should see the current time in HH:MM:SS format, such as 18:31:00:.

3. To display the time in 12-hour format with AM and PM indicators, type **PS1='\@:'** and press **Enter**. You should see the current time in HH:MM:SS format, such as 06:31PM:. Notice that the AM or PM indicator replaces the seconds display.

4. Most people want the BASH prompt to display the current directory. You can use \w to display the entire path or \W to display just the directory name. Type **PS1= '\w: '** and press **Enter**. If your current directory is your home directory, you see the ~: prompt.

5. Type **cd /usr/sbin** and press **Enter**. You should see /usr/sbin: as the prompt.

6. Type **PS1='\W:'** and press **Enter**. The prompt changes to sbin: to display only the current directory's name.

7. You can customize other BASH prompts: PS2, PS3, and PS4. The PS2 prompt is used as the secondary prompt. To see how it's used, type **echo 'Hello** (omitting the closing quote) and press **Enter**. The greater-than symbol (>) is displayed, indicating that BASH is waiting for you to complete the command.

 The PS3 and PS4 prompts aren't covered in this lab.

8. Type **'** (the closing quote) and press **Enter** to finish the command.

9. To change the PS2 prompt the same way, type **PS2='Finish your command:'** and press **Enter**.

10. Type **echo 'Hello** (omitting the closing quote), and press **Enter**. The next line displays the prompt Finish your command:.

7

11. Type ' (the closing quote) and press **Enter** to complete the command. The word Hello is displayed, followed by the PS1 prompt on a new line.

A useful addition to the PS2 prompt is having it produce a beep. You can do this by using the special character \a—for example, PS2='> \a'.

12. You can also display BASH prompts in color by adding color-setting attributes. In the following examples, the BASH prompt is set to \w\$, which simply displays the current directory followed by $ (or # if you're logged in as root). To set the prompt to blue, type **PS1='\033[0;34m\w\$ \033[0;37m'** and press **Enter**. The 34 in this command controls the color.

Make sure you use single quotes rather than double quotes in these steps to prevent BASH from attempting to expand variables.

13. If you change the number in the previous command, you get a different color. Press the **up arrow** to repeat the previous command, and press the **left arrow** until the cursor is on the m after the 34. Press the **backspace** key, and then type **1** and press **Enter**. You have changed the 34 to 31, and the prompt is now red.

Here are some color values you can experiment with: 30 = black, 31 = red, 32 = green, 34 = blue, 35 = purple, 36 = cyan, and 37 = white. Remember that you can press the up arrow to recall the command with the BASH history feature, and then modify just the number for the color attribute.

14. You can also use multiple colors for a prompt. For example, to display the current directory in red and the $ character in green, type **PS1='\033[0;31m\w\033[0;32m\$ \033[0;37m'** and press **Enter**.

15. You can control other visual attributes of shell prompts, such as brightness, blinking, and reverse video. The most useful is the brightness attribute. To make the prompt brighter (although your display hardware might make it difficult to see a substantial change in brightness), type **PS1='\033[1;31m\w\033[1;32m\$ \033[0;37m'** and press **Enter**.

16. The brightness attribute is controlled by the number 1 (after the first bracket, [) in the previous command. If you change the number, you get a different visual attribute. For example, to get reverse video, type **PS1='\033[7;31m\w\033[7;32m\$ \033[0;37m'** and press **Enter**. As you can see, the cell background is displayed in the specified color, which is red, and the character is black in the cell.

17. For a blinking prompt, type **PS1='\033[5;31m\w\033[5;32m\$ \033[0;37m'** and press **Enter**. To return to a normal prompt, type **PS1='\w:'** and press **Enter**.

18. Press **Ctrl+Alt+F1** to return to the graphical screen. If you plan to continue to the next lab, stay logged in; otherwise, shut down your computer.

Review Questions

1 Which special character displays the system time in a 24-hour format (HH:MM:SS)?

  a. `\T`

  b. `\t`

  c. `\r`

  d. `\R`

2. Which special character displays the entire directory path in the prompt?

  a. `\w`

  b. `\W`

  c. `/p`

  d. `/P`

3. The PS2 prompt is displayed when:

  a. You're in a subshell.

  b. You're using a shell other than BASH.

  c. You haven't finished typing a command, but you press the Enter key.

  d. You press the Tab key.

4. Which command produces a beep when the PS2 prompt is displayed?

  a. `PS1='\w\$'`

  b. `PS2='> \a'`

  c. `PS1='\u.\h.\w'`

  d. `PS2='> '--beep`

5. Which command displays the prompt with the entire directory path followed by the time in 12-hour format?

  a. `PS1='\t\W:'`

  b. `PS1='\w\T:'`

  c. `PS1='\w\@:'`

  d. `PS1='\@\W:'`

Lab 7.4 Adding Automation to the BASH Prompt

Objectives

The goal of this lab is to learn how to configure BASH to run shell scripts automatically.

Materials Required

This lab requires the following:

- A computer running Fedora 13 Linux

Estimated completion time: 15 minutes

Activity Background

In this lab, you build a list of people's names that's stored in a file called `list`. Each name is followed by a simple number to represent some information, such as an index to another file or database. Also, each time you add a new name to the list, you want it sorted in alphabetical order. There are many ways to do this, of course.

You also use a BASH feature that enables you to run a program automatically whenever the PS1 prompt is displayed. It's the main prompt that appears when control is returned to the BASH shell. This feature isn't available in all shells.

Activity

1. Switch to a command-line terminal (`tty2`) by pressing **Ctrl+Alt+F2**, and if necessary, log in to the terminal with any username.

2. Go to your home directory, if necessary. Use the **touch** command to create a file named `list`.

3. First, you create a simple shell script to sort the `list` file. You could use a text editor to create it, but because it's only one line, use the `echo` command. Type **echo 'sort ~/list > ~/r13; mv ~/r13 ~/list' > ~/sorter** and press **Enter** to create a script file named `sorter` in your home directory.

4. To give the script execute permission so that it can run, type **chmod +x sorter** and press **Enter**.

 Normally, programs should be placed in a suitable directory, not your home directory. In Chapter 4, you learned about the Filesystem Hierarchy Standard, so you should have some idea of which directories to use. For simplicity in this lab, however, you put the script in your home directory.

5. Next, to have BASH run the `sorter` script every time the PS1 prompt is displayed, you need to create an environment variable called `PROMPT_COMMAND` with the script name as its value. Type **PROMPT_COMMAND=~/sorter** and press **Enter**.

6. Type **echo 'Smith, John:13001'>>list** and press **Enter** to add the string `Smith, John:13001` to the end of the file.

7. Type **cat list** and press **Enter** to display the contents of the `list` file. At this point, the file has only one line, so you can't determine whether it's sorted.

8. Repeat the command in Step 6 several times, using the following information in place of `Smith, John:13001` and pressing **Enter** after each line:

   ```
   Reagan, Ronald:13002
   Clinton, Bill:13003
   Kennedy, John:13004
   ```

9. Use the **cat** command to display the contents of the `list` file. The names should be alphabetized, even though you didn't enter them in alphabetical order. The file is sorted each time BASH displayed the PS1 prompt.

10. It's unlikely you want BASH to alphabetize files all the time, so you probably don't want to put the `PROMPT_COMMAND=~/sorter` statement in a shell configuration file, such as `.bashrc`. When you want BASH to stop running the `sorter` script, you can enter

PROMPT_COMMAND= or log out and log in again. Type **PROMPT_COMMAND=** and press **Enter** to remove this environment variable.

11. Type **echo 'Lincoln, Abraham:13006'>>list** and press **Enter**. Use the **cat** command again to display this file's contents. The last name you entered, Abraham Lincoln, should remain at the end of the file instead of being sorted.

12. Press **Ctrl+Alt+F1** to return to the graphical screen. If you plan to continue to the next lab, stay logged in; otherwise, shut down your computer.

Review Questions

1. What must you do to make sure a shell script can run?

   a. After creating the shell script, log out and log in again.

   b. Make sure the /bin/bash file has the execute permission.

   c. Make sure the shell script has the execute permission assigned.

   d. Log in as the root user.

2. What's the name of the main BASH prompt?

   a. PS1

   b. PS2

   c. Prompt

   d. Prompt1

3. How do you configure BASH to run a program or command whenever the main prompt is displayed?

   a. Put a PROMPT_COMMAND statement in one of the BASH configuration files.

   b. Create the PROMPT_COMMAND environment variable and set its value to the name of the program or command you want to run.

   c. You must run another copy of the BASH shell by using the --run option.

   d. You must include the program or command's name in the PS1 environment variable's value.

4. If you want BASH to stop running a program or command when the prompt is displayed, type PROMPT_COMMAND= and press Enter. True or False?

5. Being able to run a program or command automatically when the shell prompt is displayed is a feature of all shells, not just BASH. True or False?

Lab 7.5 Setting CDPATH

Objectives

The goal of this lab is to explore using the BASH feature called CDPATH. It does for the cd command what the shell's PATH feature does for running programs: It searches for the correct directory.

Materials Required

This lab requires the following:

- A computer running Fedora 13 Linux

Estimated completion time: 15 minutes

Activity

1. Switch to a command-line terminal (tty2) by pressing **Ctrl+Alt+F2**, and if necessary, log in to the terminal with any username.

2. Make sure your current directory is your home directory. If necessary, type **cd** and press **Enter** to go to your home directory.

3. Set the BASH PS1 prompt to display the current directory's name. If you forgot how to do this, see Step 4 of Lab 7.3.

4. Type **cd bin** and press **Enter**. You see the following error message because there's no bin directory below your home directory:

   ```
   bash: cd: bin: No such file or directory
   ```

5. Type **CDPATH=:/usr** and press **Enter** to have BASH look for a subdirectory below the /usr directory if it can't find a subdirectory below the current directory.

6. Type **cd bin** and press **Enter**. This time, there's no error message. Instead, your current directory is changed to /usr/bin.

7. Go back to your home directory. Type **mkdir ~/bin** and press **Enter** to create a bin directory below your home directory.

8. Type **cd bin** and press **Enter**. This time, the current directory is set to ~/bin (the bin directory below your home directory).

9. Type **CDPATH=/usr** and press **Enter**. Notice that the colon in Step 5's similar command has been eliminated. You see the results in the next step.

10. Go back to your home directory. Type **cd bin** and press **Enter**. The current directory is set to /usr/bin, which is the bin directory below the /usr directory, not the bin directory below your home directory. What happened? Eliminating the colon specified not searching for directories below your current directory (in this case, your home directory).

 The CDPATH feature doesn't search for directories if you use a cd command that specifies a directory beginning with a slash (/), a dot (.), or two dots (..).

11. Go back to your home directory, and then type **cd ~/bin** and press **Enter**. This time, BASH sets the current directory to the ~/bin directory because you specified it. BASH didn't have to search for it.

12. Next, make the search more complex by typing **CDPATH=:/usr:/var** and pressing **Enter**. Now BASH searches your current directory first, then the /usr directory, and then the /var directory.

13. Go back to your home directory. Type **cd log** and press **Enter**. The current directory is set to /var/log. BASH can't find a log directory below the current directory or the /usr directory but does find a log directory below /var.

14. Shut down your computer.

Review Questions

1. You've entered the command CDPATH=:/usr:/var. In what order does BASH search for directories?

    a. It searches the /usr directory and then the /var directory.

    b. It searches the /var directory and then the /usr directory.

    c. It searches the current directory, then the /usr directory, and then the /var directory.

    d. It searches the /var directory, then the /usr directory, and then the current directory.

2. What problem might you encounter if you use the command CDPATH=/usr?

    a. It conflicts with PATH.

    b. BASH doesn't look for directories below your current directory.

    c. You can't make the /usr directory the current directory.

    d. It makes /usr your current directory at all times.

3. If you issue the command CDPATH=/usr and your current directory is your home directory, you can go to the bin directory under your home directory by entering cd bin. True or False?

4. If you're logged in as root and your current directory is your home directory, when you issue the command CDPATH=/usr, you can go to the /bin directory by entering cd ../bin. True or False?

5. If you issue the command CDPATH=/usr and your current directory is your home directory, you can go to the bin directory below your home directory by entering cd ~/bin. True or False?

7

CHAPTER 8

SYSTEM INITIALIZATION AND X WINDOW

Labs included in this chapter

- Lab 8.1 Setting the Initial Runlevel
- Lab 8.2 Modifying Keys
- Lab 8.3 Running an X Server
- Lab 8.4 Configuring X Programs

CompTIA Linux+ Exam Objectives

Objective		Lab
101.3	Change runlevels and shut down or reboot system	8.1, 8.2
103.1	Work on the command line	8.1, 8.2, 8.3
106.1	Install and configure X11	8.3, 8.4
106.2	Set up a display manager	8.4

Lab 8.1 Setting the Initial Runlevel

Objectives

The purpose of this lab is to learn how to change the default runlevel at startup. Many Linux distributions set the initial runlevel to 5, which starts the GUI automatically. Some Linux users prefer to have the system boot to a command prompt, however, and runlevel 3 does this. You can configure runlevels easily by modifying the /etc/inittab file. In this lab, you experiment with setting runlevels, including not specifying a runlevel at all.

Materials Required

This lab requires the following:

- A computer running Fedora 13 Linux

Estimated completion time: 15 minutes

Activity Background

The common runlevels and their meanings are as follows:

- *0*—Halt the system.
- *1*—Use single-user mode.
- *2*—Use multiuser mode but no networking support.
- *3*—Use multiuser mode with full networking support.
- *5*—Use multiuser mode with full networking support and start the graphical user interface.
- *6*—Reboot the system.

Activity

1. Switch to a command-line terminal (tty2) by pressing **Ctrl+Alt+F2**, and log in to the terminal as root.

2. Next, you edit the /etc/inittab file in any text editor. Locate the statement id:5:initdefault:, which tells init to start Linux in runlevel 5 when the computer boots. It loads the graphical subsystem before the login prompt. To change the runlevel to 3, modify the line to **id:3:initdefault:**, and then save the file and exit the editor.

3. Restart the computer by pressing **Ctrl+Alt+Del**. When the kernel is finished loading, it starts the init program, which reads the /etc/inittab file and begins performing the actions it finds there. The statement you modified tells init to start in runlevel 3, so it doesn't start the GUI. Instead, you see a text-mode login prompt. Log in as root.

4. Edit the /etc/inittab file again. To see what happens if you don't specify what runlevel to use, change the same statement to a comment by adding the # symbol at the beginning of the line, as shown here:

   ```
   #id:3:initdefault:
   ```

5. Save the file and exit the text editor.

6. Restart the computer by pressing **Ctrl+Alt+Del**. When the kernel is finished loading, `init` reads the `/etc/inittab` file and begins performing the actions it finds there. In some Linux distributions, you're prompted for the runlevel; however, Fedora 13 defaults to runlevel 3 and you're prompted to log in. Log in as root.

7. Finally, edit the `/etc/inittab` file by setting the runlevel back to **5** (and removing the # character) so that the system starts in the GUI. If you're running your computer as a desktop, it makes sense to set the initial runlevel to 5. If you're running your computer as a server, setting the initial runlevel to 3 is more useful.

8. Press **Ctrl+Alt+F1** to return to the graphical screen. If you plan to continue to the next lab, stay logged in; otherwise, shut down your computer.

Review Questions

1. The initial runlevel is set in which file?
   a. `/etc/lilo.conf` or `/etc/grub.conf`
   b. `/etc/inittab`
   c. `/etc/runlevel`
   d. `/etc/boot.conf`

2. What happens if there's no initial runlevel statement in the configuration file?
   a. The OS refuses to load, and the system hangs.
   b. The OS loads, but the `init` program hangs.
   c. The OS loads, and the `init` program prompts you for the runlevel.
   d. The OS loads, and the `init` program defaults to runlevel 3.

3. Which runlevel starts the system in multiuser mode but has no networking support?

4. Which runlevel halts the system?

5. When does it make the most sense to set the runlevel to 3 in `inittab`?

Lab 8.2 Modifying Keys

Objectives

In this lab, you learn to reconfigure the shutdown key sequence (Ctrl+Alt+Delete) so that it halts the computer instead of its usual action: restarting the computer. Restarting isn't required after most configuration changes in Linux. After you redefine the Ctrl+Alt+Delete key combination, you change the key combination that causes the shutdown process by modifying the keyboard map file.

Materials Required

This lab requires the following:

• A computer running Fedora 13 Linux

Estimated completion time: 45 minutes

Activity Background

The keyboard map is a text file in standard format, but it's not in the same location in all Linux distributions. Red Hat Linux and Fedora Core 2 place it in /lib/kbd/keymaps/ i386/qwerty/ if you're using a PC. Slackware places it in /usr/share/kbd/keymaps/ i386/qwerty/, and other distributions place it different directories. The program that reads the keyboard map file, loadkeys, includes the correct directory, so you don't have to specify it. This directory contains many keyboard map files for different physical keyboard layouts, usually for different countries and languages. The filenames give you a clue to the language or country. For example, the keyboard map for the United States is us.map in Fedora 13. Other Linux distributions use different names. Regardless of the filenames, most distributions compress these files, so you'll probably find us.map.gz instead of us.map. The loadkeys program can read the file whether it's compressed or not.

Activity

1. Switch to a command-line terminal (tty2) by pressing **Ctrl+Alt+F2**, and log in to the terminal as root.

2. First, open the /etc/init/control-alt-delete.conf file. Find the line that looks similar to exec /sbin/shutdown -r now "Control-Alt-Delete pressed". The shutdown command's -r option specifies restarting the system. To change the command so that your computer halts instead of restarting, edit the line to use the -h (halt) option instead of the -r option, as shown:

   exec /sbin/shutdown **-h** now "Control-Alt-Delete pressed"

3. Save the file and exit the editor.

4. The init program doesn't recognize the change automatically. You can restart the computer to have it reread the files init runs, including inittab and files in the /etc/init directory, but there's a quicker way. Type **kill -HUP 1** and press **Enter**. The init program rereads inittab and other files, including the control-alt-delete.conf file, and is now reconfigured to halt instead of restart on shutdown.

5. Press **Ctrl+Alt+Del**. Your computer shuts down and halts instead of restarting. If your computer has power management and your Linux distribution supports it, your computer shuts itself off.

6. Power on your computer and start Linux. Switch to a command-line terminal (tty2) by pressing **Ctrl+Alt+F2**, and log in to the terminal as root.

7. Next, you change the key combination that shuts down your computer to Ctrl+Alt+Page Up instead of Ctrl+Alt+Delete. To do this, you have to modify the keyboard map file. First, you need to find the keycode for Ctrl+Alt+Page Up by typing **showkey** and pressing **Enter**. You see a prompt that tells you to press any key; it also states that the program terminates 10 seconds after the last keypress.

It's important to enter the showkey command in a virtual console. Don't use it in an xterm session (explained in Lab 8.3).

8. Press the **Page Up** key. You see the following output:

```
keycode 104 press
keycode 104 release
```

This `showkey` output tells you that the keycode for the Page Up key is 104. In about 10 seconds, the shell prompt returns.

 Your keyboard might have two Page Up keys: one grouped with Home and End (keycode 104) and one on the numeric keypad (keycode 73). Choose the one with keycode 104.

9. The keyboard map file is `/lib/kbd/keymaps/i386/qwerty/us.map.gz`. Before you can edit this file, you have to uncompress it by typing **gunzip /lib/kbd/keymaps/i386/qwerty/us.map.gz** and pressing **Enter**.

10. To edit the file now called `/lib/kbd/keymaps/i386/qwerty/us.map`, add **control alt keycode 104 = Boot** on a separate line at the end of the file. Save the file and exit the editor. For the change to take effect, you must reload the keyboard map by typing **loadkeys us** and pressing **Enter**.

11. Shut down your computer by pressing **Ctrl+Alt+Page Up**. Start your computer again, switch to a command-line terminal (`tty2`) by pressing **Ctrl+Alt+F2**, and log in to the terminal as root.

12. By modifying the keyboard map, you made the Ctrl+Alt+Page Up key combination shut down your computer. To find out whether the Ctrl+Alt+Delete key combination still shuts down your computer, press **Ctrl+Alt+Delete**. This key combination should still work.

13. Power on your computer, and start Linux again. Switch to a command-line terminal (`tty2`) by pressing **Ctrl+Alt+F2**, and log in to the terminal as root.

14. You can prevent Ctrl+Alt+Delete from shutting down the computer by modifying the keyboard map file. The keycode for the Delete key is 111. (You could use `showkey` if you didn't know the keycode.) Edit the `/lib/kbd/keymaps/i386/qwerty/us.map` file and set the key combination to do nothing by adding **control alt keycode 111 = nul** in a separate line at the end of the file. Save the file and exit the editor.

15. To reload the keyboard map for the change to take effect, type **loadkeys us** and press **Enter**. Next, press **Ctrl+Alt+Delete**. Your computer doesn't shut down because you disabled Ctrl+Alt+Delete.

16. To restore your computer to its state before this lab, edit the keyboard map file to remove the lines you added. Then reload the keyboard map by typing **loadkeys us** and pressing **Enter**. Press **Ctrl+Alt+Delete** to make sure this key combination functions as it did originally.

17. Press **Ctrl+Alt+F1** to return to the graphical screen. If you plan to continue to the next lab, stay logged in; otherwise, shut down your computer.

8

Review Questions

1. What happens by default when you press the Ctrl+Alt+Delete key combination?

    a. The computer restarts.

    b. The computer shuts down and halts.

    c. You're logged out of the terminal or virtual console.

    d. The X Server session terminates.

2. Which file do you modify to make the Ctrl+Alt+Delete key combination perform a different action?

    a. `/etc/lilo.conf` or `/etc/grub.conf`

    b. `/etc/init/control-alt-delete.conf`

    c. `/etc/inittab`

    d. `/etc/loadkeys`

3. What's the quickest way to have modifications to the `/etc/inittab` file take effect?

    a. Press Ctrl+Alt+Delete.

    b. Press Ctrl+Alt+Backspace.

    c. Type `shutdown -r now`.

    d. Type `kill -HUP 1`.

4. Which command tells you the keycode for a key?

    a. `scankey`

    b. `showkey`

    c. `showcode`

    d. `reveal_codes`

5. Which command makes changes to the keyboard map take effect immediately?

    a. `loadkeys us`

    b. `kill -HUP init`

    c. `kill -HUP loadkeys`

    d. `shutdown -r now`

Lab 8.3 Running an X Server

Objectives

Gnome and KDE are Linux graphical desktop environments with features similar to those in Macintosh and Windows. These environments are complex, with layers of software and settings for each layer. In this lab, you run only one of these layers—the X Server program. You see what functions an X server provides and how to interact with an X server to run applications.

You might think running an X server isn't useful, but using it without the other layers of a graphical desktop environment can reduce system resource requirements and lock down a desktop so that users can run only authorized applications. You could use this technique for building a kiosk application, for example. After finishing this lab, you'll be able to do the following:

- Start and stop an X server.
- Run X applications from the command line.
- Specify command-line options to set window properties.

Materials Required

This lab requires the following:

- A computer running Fedora 13 Linux
- The basic X Window programs xcalc and xterm

Ask your instructor how to install xcalc and xterm before starting this lab.

Estimated completion time: 45 minutes

Activity

1. This lab works best with your computer configured for runlevel 3. Using a text editor (and referring to Lab 8.1, if needed), modify the /etc/inittab file so that the initdefault line is set to 3, as shown:

   id:**3**:initdefault:

2. Save the file and exit the editor.

3. Restart the computer. When you see a text-mode login prompt, log in as root.

4. The X Server program is a file called Xorg in the /usr/X11R6/bin directory, but there's also a symbolic link to it called X. To start X Server, type **X** and press **Enter**. (Make sure you type an uppercase X.) You should see some flashing text, followed by a blank screen, and then a mouse cursor.

If the screen is blank and you don't see a cursor, just skip to Step 6 to exit X Server.

5. When you move the mouse, the cursor should move. Try clicking the left mouse button, the right mouse button, and then both mouse buttons. Nothing happens.

6. Press **Ctrl+Alt+Backspace** to stop the X server and return to the virtual console, which now displays useful information about the X server, such as the server's identity and version. (This information looks different in different Linux distributions.) It also tells you that the X server is logging errors and messages to the /var/log/Xorg.0.log file and is using the /etc/X11/Xorg.conf.d file for configuration information.

8

 This information is displayed when X Server starts, not when you stop it. Because X Server displays a graphical screen immediately, you don't have an opportunity to see this information when the program starts.

7. Type **X** and press **Enter** to start X Server again.

8. Go to virtual console 1 by pressing **Ctrl+Alt+F1**. You see the same text as in Step 6. You don't see the command prompt, however, because the X server is running as a foreground process in this virtual console.

9. Press **Ctrl+C** to stop the X server and go back to the command prompt.

10. If you want to start the X server from a virtual console but run it as a background process, type **X &** and press **Enter**. Go to virtual console 1 by pressing **Ctrl+Alt+F1**. Press **Enter** once. You should see a command prompt, which means the X server is running in the background. To confirm that it's running, type **ps ax | grep X** and press **Enter**. If the X server is running, you should see output similar to the following:

```
2333 tty7    Ss+     0:02  X
```

11. You can also confirm that the X server is running by pressing **Alt+F7** to go to the X Server screen.

12. Next, you see how to run graphical programs when you have only an X server running. As you saw in Step 5, using mouse buttons doesn't display a menu or another way of choosing programs. When you have only an X server running (and no desktop manager, such as Gnome), you must start programs from a virtual console. Press **Ctrl+Alt+F1** to go to the first virtual console.

13. Start the graphical calculator program by typing **xcalc -display :0 &** and pressing **Enter**. You should see a display similar to [2] 2408 along with the command prompt. You might also see warning messages about fonts that can't be converted, but you can ignore these warnings.

14. Switch to the X Server screen by pressing **Alt+F7**. The calculator is displayed in the upper-left corner. Because it has no title bar, you can't drag the calculator window to a new position. That's because no display manager is running, only the X server.

15. If you want the calculator to be displayed somewhere else on the X server screen, you can use the -geometry option. Go back to virtual console 1 by pressing **Ctrl+Alt+F1**. To start another copy of xcalc using the -geometry option to set its size and screen position, type **xcalc -display :0 -geometry 250x320-0-0 &** and press **Enter**. This command specifies that the calculator window should be 250 pixels wide by 320 pixels high and be placed in the lower-right corner (-0-0).

16. Go to the X Server screen by pressing **Alt+F7**. The calculator window is displayed in the lower-right corner.

17. Go back to virtual console 1 by pressing **Ctrl+Alt+F1**. To stop both xcalc processes with one command, type **killall xcalc** and press **Enter**. Go back to the X Server screen by pressing **Alt+F7**, and notice that both calculator windows are gone.

18. To avoid having to switch between the X Server screen and virtual consoles by using an Alt key combination, you can make a command prompt available in the X Server screen.

Return to the virtual console by pressing **Ctrl+Alt+F1**, and then run a graphical terminal program (xterm) by typing **xterm -display :0 &** and pressing **Enter**.

19. Go to the X Server screen by pressing **Alt+F7**. The xterm window is in the upper-left corner, and you have a command prompt you can use to run programs. Move the mouse cursor over the xterm window, type **ls**, and press **Enter** to see a listing of the current directory.

20. Open another xterm window in the lower-left corner by typing **xterm -geometry 40x10+0-0 &** and pressing **Enter**.

When you start an application in an xterm window, you don't have to specify the -display option because xterm sets the DISPLAY environment variable when it loads. The application uses the value in the DISPLAY variable unless you override it with the -display option.

21. When multiple windows occupy the same screen, you need some way to select one window as the active window (the one the keyboard sends keystrokes to). The active window is said to "have focus." Move the mouse cursor down slowly, and notice that when it leaves the xterm window, it changes because the xterm window has lost focus. With the mouse cursor over no window, press some keys on the keyboard. Notice that they're not displayed onscreen. No window has focus, so the keyboard isn't connected to any window.

22. Slowly move the mouse cursor over the xterm window at the lower left. Notice that the cursor changes as the mouse moves over the window. If you press keys on the keyboard, the characters are displayed in the xterm window that has focus.

23. To run any graphical application installed on your computer from an xterm window, you just put the xterm window in focus, and then enter the program name. Type **xcalc &** and press **Enter** to start the calculator. Exit the calculator by typing **killall xcalc** and pressing **Enter**.

24. Put one of the xterm windows in focus, and then type **firefox &** and press **Enter** to start the Firefox Web browser. To exit this program, click **File, Quit** from the menu.

25. Leave your computer as is for the next lab.

Review Questions

1. When no window has focus, the keyboard is connected to the first window that was opened. True or False?

2. When you run only an X server, you can display a menu by right-clicking the desktop. True or False?

3. Which key sequence stops the X Server program?

   a.   Alt+F7

   b.   Ctrl+Alt+F7

   c.   Ctrl+Alt+Backspace

   d.   Ctrl+Alt+Esc

4. Which command-line option specifies an application's window size and location onscreen?

   a.   `-location`

   b.   `-size`

   c.   `-geometry`

   d.   `-display`

5. Moving the mouse cursor over a window makes it the active window, which means which of the following?

   a.   The program running in the active window has the highest privilege level, so programs in other windows run slower.

   b.   The keyboard is logically connected to the window.

   c.   The window can be resized.

   d.   The window remains the active window (retains focus) even if the mouse cursor leaves the window.

Lab 8.4 Configuring X Programs

Objectives

X programs (X clients) use X libraries, so they usually recognize the same command-line options, such as those for changing a window's foreground and background colors, setting transparent backgrounds, running programs that are minimized automatically, setting titles in title bars, and so forth. Not all programs use all these options, and options might be implemented in different ways. Some programs might also have unique options. In this lab, you try numerous options and see the effects.

Materials Required

This lab requires the following:

- A computer running Fedora 13 Linux
- Completion of Lab 8.3

Estimated completion time: 30 minutes

Activity

1. Go to the X Server screen by pressing **Alt+F7**. Give an xterm window focus and start the Metacity window manager (the default in Gnome) by typing **metacity &** and pressing **Enter**. Notice that the xterm window has a title bar and controls for minimizing, maximizing, and exiting. You can also move the window onscreen.

2. To start the xcalc program with a title different from the default "Calculator," type **xcalc -title "*YourName*'s Calculator" &** and press **Enter** (replacing *YourName* with your first name). The calculator opens with your name in the title bar. Exit the calculator.

3. Start the calculator again, but this time, specify a red window background by typing **xcalc -bg red &** and pressing **Enter**. (The -bg option specifies the background color.) Exit the calculator.

4. Start the calculator again, but specify a red window background and a yellow foreground (the -fg option) by typing **xcalc -bg red -fg yellow &** and pressing **Enter**. Exit the calculator.

5. Many X programs have unique command-line options. A good example is xterm's -b option that sets an inner margin. Make the xterm window active, and then type **xterm -b 50 &** and press **Enter**. The xterm window is displayed with a 50-pixel border between the window border and the text in the window.

6. Close all windows and exit to the virtual console by pressing **Ctrl+Alt+Backspace**. Shut down your computer.

Review Questions

1. Which xterm command do you use to add title bars and controls to windows?

    a. xterm -showtitles

    b. X titlebars

    c. metacity

    d. winman

2. What type of program should you use in X Window to display title bars in windows?

    a. Desktop manager

    b. Title manager

    c. X.org manager

    d. Window manager

3. Which command-line option is used to set a window's foreground color?

    a. -display

    b. -fg

    c. -bg

    d. -color

8

4. Which of the following closes all windows and exits to the virtual console?

    a.   Ctrl+Alt+Backspace

    b.   Ctrl+Shift+End

    c.   `exit`

    d.   `quit`

5. Which option do you use to set the title on a program's title bar?

    a.   `/"title goes here"`

    b.   `-show "title goes here"`

    c.   `-title "title goes here"`

    d.   `-titlebar "title goes here"`

CHAPTER 9

MANAGING LINUX PROCESSES

Labs included in this chapter

- Lab 9.1 Displaying Parent-Child Relationships Between Processes
- Lab 9.2 Customizing `ps` Output
- Lab 9.3 Writing a Shell Script with an Infinite Loop
- Lab 9.4 Experimenting with Scheduling Priorities

CompTIA Linux+ Exam Objectives

Objective		Lab
103.1	Work on the command line	9.1–9.4
103.5	Create, monitor, and kill processes	9.1–9.4
103.6	Modify process execution priorities	9.4
105.2	Customize or write simple scripts	9.3

Lab 9.1 Displaying Parent-Child Relationships Between Processes

Objectives

The goal of this lab is to investigate methods for displaying parent-child relationships between processes.

Materials Required

This lab requires the following:

- A computer running Fedora 13 Linux

Estimated completion time: 15 minutes

Activity Background

Chapter 9 in the accompanying textbook explains parent and child processes and how to use the ps -f command to see PID and PPID values. A PPID is the PID of a parent process. Using PPID values, you can see the parents of all processes. When child processes have children, the relationships are more complex and difficult to see in the display. In this lab, you explore other commands that more clearly show the relationships between processes.

Activity

1. Start your Linux computer. Switch to a command-line terminal (tty2) by pressing **Ctrl+Alt+F2**, and log in to the terminal as a regular user.

2. Type **ps -eH | more** and press **Enter**. The e option selects all processes, and the H option produces a process hierarchy display. Child processes are listed under their parents and indented by two spaces so that you can see parent-child relationships more easily than with nonhierarchical ps commands. Here's an example of what the output looks like:

   ```
   PID   TTY   TIME      CMD
   1     ?     00:00:04  init
   491   ?     00:00:02    udevd
   970   ?     00:00:00    udevd
   971   ?     00:00:00    udevd
   1141  ?     00:00:28    auditd
   1143  ?     00:00:01    audispd
   1144  ?     00:00:00    sedispatch
   1168  ?     00:00:00    rsyslogd
   ```

   If you see the --More-- prompt, press **q** to return to the command prompt.

3. Type **ps -exf | more** and press **Enter**. You see output similar to the preceding example. These options cause ps to use the \ and _ characters instead of spaces to show parent-child relationships. If you see the --More-- prompt, press **q** to return to the command prompt.

4. Type **pstree | more** and press **Enter** to see all processes on your system arranged in a parent-child hierarchy, with parent processes to the left. The following example shows that the init process is the parent (ancestor) of all other processes. Some children of init have child processes, too. For example, the login process has a bash process as its child, as shown:

```
init-+-another_clock_a |-atd
     |-log in---bash-+-more
     |                 '-pstree
```

If you see the `--More--` prompt, press **q** to return to the command prompt.

5. Type **pstree | grep mingetty** and press **Enter** to see a list of all `mingetty` processes (virtual consoles) running on your system. Instead of these processes being listed on separate lines, they're grouped on one line preceded by a number specifying how many processes are running, as shown in this example:

```
|-5*[mingetty]
```

6. Normally, `pstree` doesn't show PIDs for processes. If you need to see them, use the `-p` option by typing **pstree -p | more** and pressing **Enter**. PIDs are shown in parentheses next to process names.

7. If you plan to continue to the next lab, stay logged in to the terminal session; otherwise, shut down the computer.

Review Questions

1. Which command shows parent-child process relationships by indenting child processes?

   a. `ps -eH`

   b. `ps -exf`

   c. `ps aux`

   d. `ps -p`

2. Which column in `ps` output identifies parent processes?

   a. PID

   b. PPID

   c. TTY

   d. COMMAND

3. Which process is the parent or ancestor of all other processes?

   a. `ps`

   b. `init`

   c. `login`

   d. `startx`

4. To see all system processes, you must be logged in as root. True or False?

5. PIDS of processes are always displayed when you use the `pstree` command. True or False?

Lab 9.2 Customizing `ps` Output

Objectives

The goal of this lab is to learn how to use the `ps` command to customize process display formats. Standard display formats are designed for general use and usually show more information than needed, but you can use command-line options to modify what information is displayed.

Materials Required

This lab requires the following:

- A computer running Fedora 13 Linux

Estimated completion time: 15 minutes

Activity

1. If necessary, start your Linux computer, switch to a command-line terminal, and log in to the terminal with a regular user account.

2. Type **ps -e | more** and press **Enter**. The -e option displays all processes. The output has four columns: PID, TTY, TIME, and CMD. The first few lines of output look similar to the following:

```
PID TTY   TIME      CMD
1   ?     00:00:04  init
2   ?     00:00:02  kthreadd
3   ?     00:00:00  migration/0
4   ?     00:00:00  ksoftirqd/0
```

If you see the --More-- prompt at the bottom, press **q** to get back to the command prompt.

3. Type **ps ax | more** and press **Enter**. The a option displays all processes started by a terminal (tty), and the x option displays all processes not started by a terminal. Using these two options together is the logical equivalent of the -e option. This display has five columns: PID, TTY, STAT, TIME, and COMMAND. There are also subtle differences in how data is displayed; for example, child processes are shown in brackets. The first few lines of output look similar to the following:

```
PID TTY   STAT  TIME  COMMAND
1   ?     Ss    0:04  /sbin/init
2   ?     S     0:02  [kthreadd]
3   ?     S     0:00  [migration/0]
```

If you see the --More-- prompt at the bottom, press **q** to go back to the command prompt.

4. To see more options for changing the format, type **ps -ef | more** and press **Enter**. The -ef option displays all processes in a full listing format, as you can see in this example:

```
UID   PID  PPID  C  STIME  TTY  TIME      CMD
root  1    0     0  Oct08  ?    00:00:04  /sbin/init
root  2    1     0  Oct08  ?    00:00:02  [kthreadd]
root  3    1     0  Oct08  ?    00:00:00  [migration/0]
root  4    0     0  Oct08  ?    00:00:00  [ksoftirqd/0]
```

If you see the --More-- prompt at the bottom, press **q** to go back to the command prompt.

5. Try the following display formats and notice how each one is displayed:

- -f—Full listing
- -j—Jobs format

- j—Job control format
- l—Long listing
- s—Signal format
- v—Virtual memory format
- x—i386 register format (use only with an Intel processor-based system)

6. The -o option is for a user-defined format. Type **ps -eo pid,cmd | more** and press **Enter** to specify showing only the PID and CMD columns, as in this example:

```
PID   CMD
  1   /sbin/init
  2   [kthreadd]
  3   [migration/0]
```

You must have a space after the -o option and no spaces before or after the commas separating column names.

If you see the --More-- prompt at the bottom, press **q** to go back to the command prompt.

7. Type **ps -eo pid,ppid,%mem,cmd | more** and press **Enter** to add the PPID and %MEM columns to the display. (A PPID is the process ID of a parent process, as you learned in Lab 9.1.) The %mem option displays the percentage of system memory a process uses. Processes that use only a tiny portion of system memory are displayed as 0.0, as shown in this example:

```
PID   PPID   %MEM   CMD
  1    0     0.1    /sbin/init
  2    0     0.0    [kthreadd]
  3    2     0.0    [migration/0]
```

Processes with PPID values of 0 have been started by the OS. Processes with PPID values of 1 have been started by init. The Linux+ Certification exam refers to these processes as "core services."

8. If you plan to continue to the next lab, press **Ctrl+Alt+F1** to return to the graphical screen; otherwise, shut down the computer.

Review Questions

1. Which command displays all processes?

a. ps

b. ps a

c. ps x

d. ps -e

9

2. Which command is equivalent to `ps -e` in terms of what processes are displayed?

   a. `ps`

   b. `ps ax`

   c. `ps -l`

   d. `ps -a`

3. Which command displays a user-defined format?

   a. `ps --option pid,cmd`

   b. `ps -options pid,cmd`

   c. `ps -o pid:cmd`

   d. `ps -o pid,cmd`

4. Which command displays the status of a process?

   a. `ps`

   b. `ps ax`

   c. `ps -l`

   d. `ps -e`

5. Which of these options should you use with a user-defined format to display the command that started the process?

   a. `com`

   b. `ppid`

   c. `cmd`

   d. `%mem`

Lab 9.3 Writing a Shell Script with an Infinite Loop

Objectives

In this lab, you write a shell script that creates an infinite loop. You use this script in subsequent labs.

Materials Required

This lab requires the following:

- A computer running Fedora 13 Linux

Estimated completion time: 10 minutes

Activity

1. Start Linux and log in to the GUI as a regular user.

2. Open a terminal window by clicking **Applications**, pointing to **System Tools**, and clicking **Terminal**. To start the gedit text editor, type **gedit loop** and press **Enter**. In gedit, type the following, pressing **Enter** after each line:

```
#!/bin/bash
while :
do
    x=1
done
```

3. Click **Save**, and then close gedit. The first line specifies that the file is a BASH script. The second line starts a `while` loop that's infinite because of the `:` at the end. The `do` and `done` lines make up the body of the loop. The `x=1` statement just gives the loop something to do; you can't have a loop with no statements in it.

4. To set the executable permission for the script, type **chmod 555 loop** at the terminal prompt and press **Enter**.

5. To test the script, type **./loop** and press **Enter**. (*Tip*: You precede the filename with `./` to specify loading the script from the current directory.) There shouldn't be any output, but the prompt doesn't return, which means the script is running. To verify, open another terminal window, and then type **ps ax | grep loop** and press **Enter**. The first line of output should look similar to the following:

```
22547  pts/0  R+  0:30  /bin/bash    ./loop
```

6. Stop the loop by typing **kill 22547** and press **Enter** (replacing 22547 with the process ID the `ps` command displayed).

7. In the first terminal window, you see the message "Terminated," and the prompt is displayed. (Instead of killing the process, you could have simply pressed Ctrl+C in the terminal window where you ran the `loop` command.) Close all terminal windows, but stay logged in for the next lab.

Review Questions

1. After you create a script, what must you do before you can run it?

   a. Compile it with `gcc`.

   b. Set the executable permission.

   c. Move the file to the `/bin` directory.

   d. Do nothing; the script is ready to run.

2. If you want to start an infinite loop in the BASH shell, which command do you use?

   a. `while :`

   b. `do until ;`

   c. `do forever`

   d. `while []`

3. If you want to see information about a process named `myproc` that was started in another terminal window, which command do you use?

   a. `ps | find myproc`

   b. `grep myproc | ps -e`

9

    c. `ps -e | locate myproc`

    d. `ps ax | grep myproc`

4. Which command do you use to run a script named `myscript` in your current directory?

    a. `run myscript`

    b. `.. myscript`

    c. `./myscript`

    d. `myscript`

5. The only way to stop an infinite loop in a BASH script is to use the `kill` command. True or False?

Lab 9.4 Experimenting with Scheduling Priorities

Objectives

The goal of this lab is to experiment with scheduling priorities by using the `nice`, `renice`, and `top` commands. Unlike most of the labs you've done so far, you use the GUI so that you can have multiple terminal windows, called `xterms`, displayed at the same time.

Materials Required

This lab requires the following:

- A computer running Fedora 13 Linux
- Completion of Lab 9.3

Estimated completion time: 30 minutes

Activity

1. Start Linux, if necessary, and log in to the GUI as a regular user.

2. To open three terminal windows on the same screen, click **Applications**, point to **System Tools**, and click **Terminal**. Repeat this step two more times. When you open the first two windows, resize each one so that it's about one inch wide. When you open the third window, make it wider—about three inches. Position the windows so that they're next to one another (see Figure 9-1).

3. In each window, type **PS1="\w:"** and press **Enter** to shorten the shell prompt so that it fits in the window. In the third window, you'll be issuing commands requiring root access, so type **su** and press **Enter** first. When prompted, type the root user's password and press **Enter**, and then enter the command for resizing the prompt.

4. Open a fourth terminal window, and then resize and position it so that the screen looks similar to Figure 9-2.

5. To perform some commands regular users can't perform, you need to log in as the root user again. In the fourth window, type **su** and press **Enter**, and then type the root user's password and press **Enter**. Next, type **top** and press **Enter**, and then type **i** so that `top` displays only active processes. Type **lmt** so that `top` no longer displays information at the top of the screen. (*Note*: This fourth terminal window is called the "top window" in these steps.)

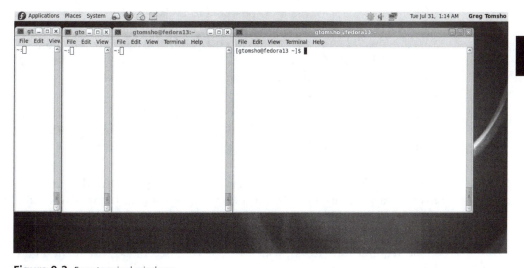

Figure 9-1 Positioning three terminal windows

Source: Fedora Linux (*http://fedoraproject.org*)

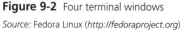

Figure 9-2 Four terminal windows

Source: Fedora Linux (*http://fedoraproject.org*)

6. In the far-left terminal window, type **./loop** and press **Enter** to run the script you created in Lab 9.3. Repeat this step in the terminal window next to it. Your screen should look similar to Figure 9-3.

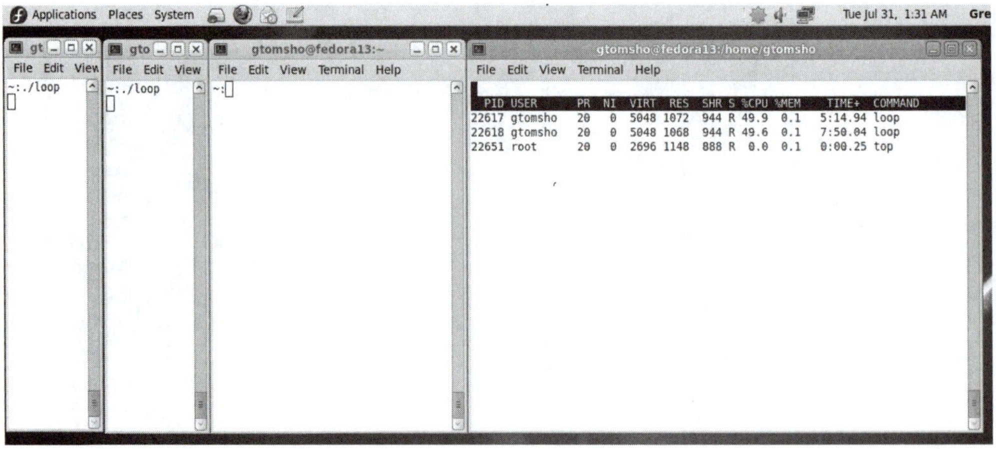

Figure 9-3 The loop script running in the top window

Source: Fedora Linux (*http://fedoraproject.org*)

7. The top window shows the two loop commands you entered as running processes with similar %CPU values, meaning both are consuming about the same amount of processing time and running at similar speeds. Write down the PIDs of these two processes, and use them in the following commands instead of *PID1* and *PID2*. Click the third window, and then type **renice 19 *PID1*** and press **Enter**. You've changed *PID1*'s scheduling priority to 19.

8. Wait a few seconds for the top command to update its display, and then look at the top window. The PR column shows 39 for *PID1* and 20 for *PID2*. The renice command added the value 19 to *PID1*, making the priority lower. The NI column shows 19 for *PID1* and 0 for *PID2*, meaning the nice value 19 has been applied to *PID1* (and *PID2* has no nice value applied). The %CPU value for *PID2* is now larger than for *PID1*, meaning *PID2* is running faster.

9. The top command includes the same function as the renice command. Click in the top window and press **r**. At the PID to renice: prompt, type *PID1* and press **Enter** (replacing *PID1* with the PID of your process). At the Renice PID PID1 to value: prompt, type **-19** and press **Enter**.

10. Wait a few seconds for top to update its display, and notice that the %CPU value for *PID1* is larger than for *PID2*, so *PID1* is now running faster than *PID2*. Notice, too, that the PR column has the value 1 for *PID1* and the NI value -19.

11. Click the third window, and type **nice -n -10 ./loop** and press **Enter**. (The nice command requires root access, which is why you used the su command in Step 3.) Wait a few seconds for the top command to update its display, and then notice that there's a third loop process. It has -10 in the NI column, which shows you can set a process's scheduling priority when you start running it.

12. Take your hands off the mouse and keyboard, and wait 10 seconds or so for the system to settle down. Notice that the top window displays other active processes besides `loop`. The `top` process is listed, but its %CPU value should be small (usually below 1.0) and consistent. You might also see processes related to the graphical desktop, such as `X.org`, `panel`, and others.

13. Quit all the `loop` commands by pressing **Ctrl+C** in each window in which `loop` is running, and then type **exit** and press **Enter** to close each terminal window. Press **q** in the top window to quit `top`, and then shut down your computer.

Review Questions

1. Which option causes `top` to display only running processes?

    a. a

    b. e

    c. i

    d. o

2. Which command can change the scheduling priority of a running process? (Choose all that apply.)

    a. top

    b. ps

    c. nice

    d. renice

3. Which of the following scheduling priority values (`nice` values) causes a process to run the fastest?

    a. 0

    b. 1

    c. -19

    d. +19

4. If you want to run commands as root, which command do you run first?

    a. root

    b. su

    c. top

    d. nice

5. A running process that `top` shows with the PR value 0 runs faster than a process with the PR value 10. True or False?

CHAPTER 10

COMMON ADMINISTRATIVE TASKS

Labs included in this chapter

- Lab 10.1 Configuring Virtual Consoles
- Lab 10.2 Testing Logging
- Lab 10.3 Using Named Pipes with Logging
- Lab 10.4 Finding Broken Links and Files with No Owners
- Lab 10.5 Understanding File Timestamps

CompTIA Linux+ Exam Objectives

Objective		Lab
103.1	Work on the command line	10.1–10.5
103.3	Perform basic file management	10.1–10.5
103.4	Use streams, pipes, and redirects	10.3
104.6	Create and change hard and symbolic links	10.4
104.5	Manage file permissions and ownership	10.4, 10.5
105.2	Customize and write simple scripts	10.3
108.2	System logging	10.2, 10.3

Lab 10.1 Configuring Virtual Consoles

Objectives
The goal of this lab is to become familiar with running a Linux computer via the command-line interface. A command-line interface is useful when the computer functions as a server. In this lab, you learn how to do the following:

- Start the computer in a different runlevel.
- Increase the number of virtual consoles.
- Move between virtual consoles.

Materials Required
This lab requires the following:

- A computer running Fedora 13 Linux

Estimated completion time: 20 minutes

Activity
1. Start your Linux computer. Switch to a command-line terminal (tty2) by pressing **Ctrl+Alt+F2**, and log in to the terminal as root.

2. To configure the computer to start in runlevel 3 instead of runlevel 5, type **vi /etc/inittab** and press **Enter**. The file's contents should be displayed. Press the **down arrow** key to move the cursor down to the id:5:initdefault: statement, and then press **i**. The bottom line changes to INSERT, indicating that you're in insert mode.

3. Delete the 5 in the id:5:initdefault: statement and replace it with a **3**, and then press the **Esc** key. INSERT is removed from the bottom line, meaning you're back in command mode. Type **:wq** and press **Enter** to save the file and exit the editor.

4. Restart the computer by typing **shutdown -r now** and pressing **Enter**. When the computer has finished restarting, you see a text-mode login prompt. Log in as the root user.

5. By default, the number of virtual consoles is set to six, but you can add more by editing the /etc/sysconfig/init file. To do this, type **vi /etc/sysconfig/init** and press **Enter**. Press the **down arrow** key until you see the line ACTIVE_CONSOLES=/dev/tty[1-6].

6. Press the **right arrow** until the cursor is over the right brace (]). Press **i**, press **Backspace**, and type **9** to change the number of virtual consoles to 9. Press **Esc**, and then type **:wq** and press **Enter** to save the file and quit vi.

7. Restart the computer by typing **shutdown -r now** and pressing **Enter**. When the system restarts, log in again as root.

8. Press **Alt+F7** or **Ctrl+Alt+F7**. Both key combinations should work, and you should see a login prompt. Log in as any user.

9. Press **Alt+F8**. When you see a login prompt, log in as any user. Press **Alt+F9**. Again, when you see a login prompt, log in as any user.

10. Type **w** and press **Enter** to see a list of all virtual consoles you're logged in to. The TTY column specifies the virtual console being used; tty1 is the first virtual console, tty2

is the second, and so on. Being logged in to all virtual consoles looks similar to the following:

```
1:57pm  up 1:21,   9 users, load average: 2.07, 2.02, 1.77
USER   TTY   FROM   LOGIN@   IDLE   JCPU    PCPU    WHAT
root   tty1  -      12:37pm  35:06  0.14s   0.14s   -bash
root   tty2  -      1:21pm   36:11  8.75s   8.69s   top
root   tty3  -      1:21pm   36:06  0.12s   0.12s   -bash
root   tty4  -      1:21pm   35:57  0.07s   0.07s   -bash
root   tty5  -      1:21pm   35:47  17:56   17:56   primes
root   tty6  -      1:22pm   35:35  17:40   17:40   primes
root   tty7  -      1:22pm   0.00s  0.13s   0.03s   w
root   tty8  -      1:23pm   34:28  0.09s   0.09s   -bash
root   tty9  -      1:23pm   34:11  0.08s   0.08s   -bash
```

You can have up to 63 virtual consoles (`tty1` to `tty63`). You can select the first 12 with Alt+F*x* (replacing *x* with one of the 12 function keys and using the left Alt key). To select the next 12, use the right Alt key. Beyond 24, you can move from one virtual console to the next with Alt+right arrow and Alt+left arrow.

From a command prompt, you can go to any virtual console by typing `chvt x` (replacing *x* with a number from 1 to 63).

11. Type **chvt 1** and press **Enter** to change to virtual console 1, and then type **chvt 8** and press **Enter** to change to virtual console 8. The `chvt` command is handy if you have a lot of virtual consoles open and know the number of the one you want to go to.

12. Next, you need to change the `/etc/inittab` file so that your system starts in a graphical desktop. Change to virtual console 1, where you're logged in as root. Use vi to edit the `/etc/inittab` file to restore the line you modified in Steps 2 and 3 so that it looks like this:

    id:5:initdefault:

13. Restart your computer if you plan to continue to the next lab; otherwise, shut it down.

10

Review Questions

1. Which file do you edit to change the runlevel your computer boots into?
   a. `/etc/sysconfig/init`
   b. `lilo.conf`
   c. `/etc/inittab`
   d. `/etc/rc.local`

2. Most Linux distributions have how many virtual consoles by default?
   a. 4
   b. 6
   c. 8
   d. 12

3. Which file do you edit to add virtual consoles?

   a. `/etc/sysconfig/init`

   b. `/etc/vc.conf`

   c. `/etc/inittab`

   d. `grub.conf`

4. What's the maximum number of virtual consoles?

   a. 16

   b. 32

   c. 63

   d. 64

5. Which command moves you to any virtual console?

Lab 10.2 Testing Logging

Objectives

The goal of this lab is to learn how to test the logging `rsyslog` performs to see whether it works the way you intended when you created or modified the `/etc/rsyslog.conf` file. To test logging, you must specify logging events of different services and priorities so that you can see how `rsyslog` handles them. Fortunately, most Linux distributions include the `logger` command, which makes this testing easy.

Materials Required

This lab requires the following:

- A computer running Fedora 13 Linux

  Estimated completion time: 30 minutes

Activity

1. Log in to the GUI as a regular user.

2. Open three terminal windows. (Refer to Lab 9.4 if you need a refresher on how to open a terminal window.) Size and position the three windows so that they're stacked vertically and are short but wide, as in Figure 10-1. You need root privileges in all three windows, so in each terminal window, type **su** and press **Enter**, and then type the root password and press **Enter**.

3. In the top window, type **less /etc/rsyslog.conf** and press **Enter** to display the `rsyslog.conf` file's contents. You can use the up and down arrow keys to see the entire file.

4. In the second window, type **tail -f /var/log/messages** and press **Enter** to see the last few lines of the `messages` file. The `-f` option is used with `tail` to monitor the file and display any updates onscreen.

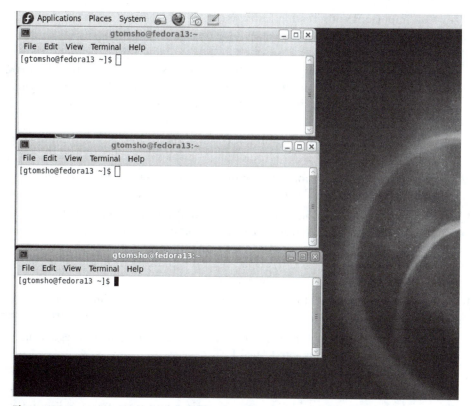

Figure 10-1   Arranging three terminal windows
Source: Fedora Linux (*http://fedoraproject.org*)

5. In the third window, type **logger -p daemon.info This is a test of daemon.info** and press **Enter** to generate a logging message for the `daemon` service with the `info` priority. A line is displayed in the second window, starting with the current date and time and followed by your computer's name, the user who logged the message, and the message text. Notice that the service and priority aren't included.

6. Type **logger -p daemon.warning This is a test of daemon.warning** and press **Enter**. You see this message in the second window.

7. Type **logger -p mail.info This is a test of mail.info** and press **Enter**. Nothing is displayed in the second window because this message is for the `mail` service. Your `rsyslog.conf` file is configured to send mail to a different log file. Click in the first window and press the **down arrow** until you find the line starting with `mail.*`. Any log messages for the `mail` service are stored in the `/var/log/maillog` file.

8. Click in the second window, and press **Ctrl+C** to return to the shell prompt. Type **tail -f /var/log/maillog** and press **Enter**. The last line of output contains the message you sent in Step 7: `This is a test of mail.info`.

9. Next, you have `rsyslog` do additional logging by sending any log messages with the `err` priority or higher to a file called `important`. To do this, click in the third window. Because `rsyslog` doesn't create the file for you, you must create it by typing **touch**

/var/log/important and pressing **Enter**. Next, type **ls -l /var/log im*** and press **Enter** to see that the file is created with a length of zero.

10. Next, you need to add a line to the `rsyslog.conf` file. Although you can use a text editor, use the `echo` command by typing **echo "*.err /var/log/important" >> /etc/rsyslog.conf** and pressing **Enter**. The `rsyslog` daemon doesn't detect this change automatically, so you must specify that its configuration file has changed by typing **killall -HUP rsyslogd** and pressing **Enter**.

11. Click in the second window, and press **Ctrl+C** to return to the shell prompt. Type **tail -f /var/log/important** and press **Enter**. Nothing is displayed because the file is empty.

12. In the third window, type **logger -p mail.err This is a test of mail.err** and press **Enter**. Notice that the message is displayed in the second window.

13. Type **logger -p mail.warning This is a test of mail.warning** and press **Enter**. Nothing is displayed in the second window because the log message was sent with the `warning` priority, which is a lower priority than `err`. Only messages with the priority `err` and higher are sent to the `/var/log/important` file. In order from lowest to highest, these priorities are `err`, `crit`, `alert`, and `emerg`.

14. Type **logger -p mail.alert This is a test of mail.alert** and press **Enter**. The message is displayed in the second window because the `alert` priority is higher than the `err` priority.

15. Open a virtual console by pressing **Ctrl+Alt+F2**, and then log in as a regular user. Switch back to the GUI by pressing **Ctrl+Alt+F1**.

16. Type **logger -p mail.emerg This is a test of mail.emerg** and press **Enter**. The message is displayed in the second window. Switch to the virtual console by pressing **Ctrl+Alt+F2**. You see the message created by `logger` because a line in the `rsyslog.conf` file sends messages with the `emerg` priority to all users on the system. The line looks like this:

```
*.emerg    *
```

17. Close all three terminal windows, and log out of the virtual console. If you plan to continue to the next lab, stay logged in; otherwise, shut down the system.

Review Questions

1. Which command displays the last few lines of the `messages` file and monitors it for changes?

   a. `head /var/log/messages`

   b. `head -f /var/log/messages`

   c. `tail /var/log/messages`

   d. `tail -f /var/log/messages`

2. Which command sends a message for the `mail` service with the `info` priority?

   a. `log mail,info This is a test`

   b. `log -p mail info This is a test`

   c. `logger -p mail.info This is a test`

   d. `logger -w mail:info This is a test`

3. If you modify `/etc/rsyslog.conf`, what command makes the changes effective without restarting the system?

4. Which of the following is the highest message priority?

   a. `crit`

   b. `alert`

   c. `debug`

   d. `warning`

5. Which statement placed in the `rsyslog.conf` file sends all messages with the `crit` priority and higher to everyone logged in?

   a. `mail.crit /var/log/everyone`

   b. `crit. **`

   c. `*.crit |/var/log`

   d. `*.crit  *`

Lab 10.3 Using Named Pipes with Logging

Objectives

The goal of this lab is to learn how to use named pipes and simple scripts to increase the capabilities of system logging. It's not uncommon for a Linux server to have two or more daemons logging to the same service. A good example is an e-mail server running SMTP and POP3 daemons. Both log to the `mail` service, so log messages for both daemons are written to the same log file. You can't configure `rsyslog` to write log messages for these two daemons to separate files. However, you can use a named pipe and a simple script to send the messages to separate files.

Materials Required

This lab requires the following:

- A computer running Fedora 13 Linux

Estimated completion time: 15 minutes

Activity

1. Log in to the GUI, if necessary, and open a terminal window. Type **su** and press **Enter**, and then enter the root password.

2. To create the files where you're going to log SMTP and POP3 messages, type **touch /var/log/smtp** and press **Enter**, and then type **touch /var/log/pop3** and press **Enter**. Type **ls -l /var/log** and press **Enter** to see that the two files have been created with zero length.

3. Next, create a named pipe so that you can use your own program to filter `rsyslogd` output by typing **mknod /var/log/mailpipe p** and pressing **Enter**. Type **ls -l /var/log/mail*** and press **Enter** to see the `mailpipe` entry in the list of files. The first character in the line is "p," which stands for "pipe."

4. Next, you use gedit or vi to add a line to the `/etc/rsyslog.conf` file so that `rsyslogd` knows to send output to the named pipe. Open the **/etc/rsyslog.conf** file, and then type **mail.* l/var/log/mailpipe** at the end of the file. Next, look for the line `mail.*`

10

`-/var/log/maillog` in the RULES section and type **#** at the beginning of this line (to "comment out" the line). `Rsyslogd` doesn't detect this change automatically. As you learned in Lab 10.2, you must specify that its configuration file has changed by typing **killall -HUP rsyslogd** and pressing **Enter**.

When you specify a named pipe in the `rsyslog.conf` file, you must precede the log file's path and name with a vertical bar (|) with no space before the file's pathname.

5. `Rsyslog` now logs messages for the `mail` service to the named pipe. However, nothing is listening to the pipe. You need to write a script to accept messages from the pipe, decide whether they're from the SMTP or POP3 daemon, and send messages to the correct file. Create a file called **mailscript** in the **/usr/local/bin** directory, and type the following shell script in gedit or vi:

```
while :
do
  read </var/log/mailpipe
  if echo $REPLY | grep "pop3" > /dev/null
  then
    echo $REPLY >> /var/log/pop3
  else
    echo $REPLY >> /var/log/smtp
  fi
done
```

This script is simple and might need some refinement if you want to use it on a real server. You can write scripts in any language, such as Perl or C.

6. To assign execute permission to the script, type **chmod +x /usr/local/bin/mailscript** and press **Enter**.

7. Run the script in the background by typing **mailscript &** and pressing **Enter**.

8. Open two other terminal windows and adjust their sizes and positions so that they look similar to Figure 10-1 in Lab 10.2. Place the window you've been using for Steps 1 through 7 at the top. It's referred to as the "first" window in subsequent steps.

9. Click in the second window, and then type **tail -f /var/log/smtp** and press **Enter**. Click in the third window, and then type **tail -f /var/log/pop3** and press **Enter**.

10. In the first window, type **logger -p mail.info This is a message from the pop3 daemon** and press **Enter**. This message is displayed in the third window because it was written to the `/var/log/pop3` log file.

11. Type **logger -p mail.info This is a message from the smtp daemon** and press **Enter**. This message is displayed in the second window.

12. Close all three terminal windows. If you plan to continue to the next lab, stay logged in; otherwise, shut down the computer.

Review Questions

1. Which command creates a named pipe in the directory where log files are placed?

   a. `mknod /var/log/logpipe p`

   b. `mknod p /var/log/logpipe`

   c. `makenode /usr/log/logpipe p`

   d. `maknod np /var/log/logpipe`

2. By default, `mail`-related messages go to which of the following files?

   a. `/log/mail`

   b. `/usr/log/allmail`

   c. `/log/var/mailmsg`

   d. `/var/log/maillog`

3. Which of the following statements in `rsyslog.conf` sends all `mail`-related messages with the `err` priority and higher to a named pipe called `mailerr` in the directory for log files?

   a. `mail.error /usr/log/mailerr`

   b. `mail.err >/var/log/mailerr`

   c. `mail.err |/var/log/mailerr`

   d. `mail.error |usr/log/mailerr`

4. Write the command to test logging `cron`-related messages with the `crit` priority.

5. Which command runs `logscript` in the background?

   a. `logscript`

   b. `logscript --background`

   c. `logscript &`

   d. `daemon logscript`

Lab 10.4 Finding Broken Links and Files with No Owners

Objectives

The goal of this lab is to learn how to find and fix files with no owners and symbolic links that no longer point to a file. Both are common system administration tasks.

Materials Required

This lab requires the following:

- A computer running Fedora 13 Linux

Estimated completion time: 15 minutes

If you already have accounts for users named Julie and Mike, substitute other names in this lab.

Activity

1. Start your Linux system, if necessary. Switch to a command-line terminal (tty2) by pressing **Ctrl+Alt+F2**, and log in to the terminal as root.

2. To create a user account to use for this lab, type **useradd julie** and press **Enter**. Log in to Julie's user account by typing **su julie** and pressing **Enter**.

When you're the root user and use the su command to become another user, you don't have to enter the user's password.

3. Go to Julie's home directory by typing **cd /home/julie** and pressing **Enter**. Type **touch file1** and press **Enter** to create a file in this directory. Create three or four more files, using whatever names you like.

4. Type **ls -l** and press **Enter** to see the files in Julie's home directory. Note that Julie is both the user owner and group owner of the files you created.

5. To make sure other users can't read files in Julie's home directory, take away their read permission by typing **chmod o-r *** and pressing **Enter**. Type **ls -l** and press **Enter** to verify that only Julie and the root user can read her files. Type **exit** and press **Enter** to log out of Julie's account. You're now logged in as root. Type **cd /home/julie** and press **Enter**.

6. To delete Julie's user account, type **userdel julie** and press **Enter**.

7. Type **ls -l** and press **Enter** to see the files in Julie's home directory. The user owner is now a number, such as 502, instead of the name "julie." The group owner is also a number because every file's owner is stored in the directory as a numeric user ID (UID). When you delete the user, the ls command displays the UID instead of the user account name because the file no longer has an owner. Here's an example of ls output for an account with no owner:

```
total 0
-rw-rw---- 1 502 502 0 Oct 22 09:48 file1
-rw-rw---- 1 502 502 0 Oct 22 09:48 file2
-rw-rw---- 1 502 502 0 Oct 22 09:48 file3
-rw-rw---- 1 502 502 0 Oct 22 09:48 file4
-rw-rw---- 1 502 502 0 Oct 22 09:48 file5
```

8. Create another user by typing **useradd mike** and pressing **Enter**. Type **ls -l** and press **Enter**. As shown, Julie's old files are now owned by Mike because useradd assigned Mike the UID that became available when Julie's user account was deleted:

```
total 0
-rw-rw---- 1 mike mike 0 Oct 22 09:48 file1
-rw-rw---- 1 mike mike 0 Oct 22 09:48 file2
-rw-rw---- 1 mike mike 0 Oct 22 09:48 file3
-rw-rw---- 1 mike mike 0 Oct 22 09:48 file4
-rw-rw---- 1 mike mike 0 Oct 22 09:48 file5
```

When you delete an existing user account and do nothing about files in this user's home directory, the files are accessible to a future user who's assigned the same UID.

9. To delete Mike's user account, type **userdel mike** and press **Enter**. Again, the files in Julie's home directory have no owner.

10. Scanning your system periodically for files with no owner tells you when files might have been abandoned. If their permissions are set to -rw-rw----, as in the previous steps, the only user who can access them is root. You might want to assign these files to another suitable user or delete them. To search the entire file system from the root directory down, type **find / -nouser** and press **Enter**. Here's an example of what might be displayed:

```
/home/julie
/home/julie/file1
/home/julie/file2
/home/julie/file3
/home/julie/file4
/home/julie/file5
/home/julie/.bash_history
. . .
```

11. To delete unowned files but be prompted to confirm the deletion of each file, type **find / -nouser -ok rm "{}" ";"** and press **Enter**. All files listed in Step 10 as well as files owned by Mike are displayed one by one, followed by a question mark prompt. You press y to delete the file or n if you don't want to delete it. Press **Ctrl+C** to exit find. You still need a few of these files in the next steps.

12. Another common administrative task is repairing or deleting broken symbolic links (also called "dangling links"), which point to files or directories that no longer exist. Unfortunately, you can't use the find command to find dangling links, but you can use symlinks. To see how it works, first type **touch /home/mike/hello** and press **Enter** to create a file in the /home/mike directory. Then type **ln -s /home/mike/hello hello** and press **Enter** to create a symbolic link to the hello file. Next, to create a dangling link, type **rm /home/mike/hello** and press **Enter**. If necessary, type y to confirm the deletion.

13. To find all dangling links, type **symlinks -r / | grep dangling** and press **Enter**. To delete all dangling links, type **symlinks -r -d /** and press **Enter**.

14. If you plan to continue to the next lab, stay logged in; otherwise, shut down the system.

10

Review Questions

1. When you're the root user and use the su command to become another user, you must enter the user's password. True or False?

2. Everyone can read and write unowned files that have -rw-rw--- permissions. True or False?

3. When you list files with the ls -l command, what's in the user and group owner columns for unowned files?

   a. The name of the most recent user owner

   b. The name of the user who created the file

   c. The root user

   d. The UID and GID of the most recent user owner

4. Which command displays all files that have no user owners in the file system?

    a. `find ./ --nouser`

    b. `find / -nouser`

    c. `locate / -no-user`

    d. `locate --nouser /`

5. Which command finds and displays any broken symbolic links in the file system?

    a. `find / --dangling`

    b. `find / -links | grep dangling`

    c. `symlinks -c /`

    d. `symlinks -r / | grep dangling`

Lab 10.5 Understanding File Timestamps

Objectives

Users save files in their home directories or use their computers as file servers, where they store files in shared directories. When free disk space diminishes to the point that system operation is jeopardized, Linux system administrators have to do file "housekeeping," which means recovering disk space by deleting or moving outdated and unnecessary files, or ask users to do their own housekeeping.

You can recover disk space by deleting old files that are no longer needed or moving old files to other media (tape, optical discs, flash drives, and so on). To identify old files, you can check their timestamps. Each file has three types of timestamps, and administrators should know how they work to help them with file-housekeeping tasks.

Materials Required

This lab requires the following:

- A computer running Fedora 13 Linux

Estimated completion time: 30 minutes

Activity Background

Linux files have three types of timestamps:

- The creation time (`ctime`) is set to the current time and date automatically when the file or directory is created. It's also changed to the current time when a file's permissions, attributes, owners, or contents change.

- The access time (`atime`) is changed to the current time and date automatically when the file is opened.

- The modification time (`mtime`) is changed when the file is written to and closed.

Activity

1. If necessary, start your system, switch to `tty2`, and log in to the terminal as root.

2. Switch to Julie's home directory (created in Lab 10.4) by typing **cd /home/julie** and pressing **Enter**.

3. To remove all files in this directory, type **rm * -I** and press **Enter**. When you're prompted with `rm: remove all arguments?`, type y and press **Enter**.

4. Create a new file called `file1` with the `touch` command. Type **ls -l** and press **Enter**. Normally, the `ls` command displays `mtime`, as shown in this example:

```
-rw-r--r--    1    root    root    0    Oct 23    08:40    file1
```

5. To display the file's `ctime`, you use the `--time` option. Type **ls -l --time=ctime** and press **Enter**. (*Note*: Make sure you use two hyphens before the `time` option.) In this example, the date and time are the same as with `mtime`:

```
-rw-r--r--    1    root    root    0    Oct 23    08:40    file1
```

6. To display a file's `atime`, type **ls -l --time=atime** and press **Enter**. As shown in this example, the `atime` is the same as the `mtime` and `ctime` values:

```
-rw-r--r--    1    root    root    0    Oct 23    08:40    file1
```

7. You can't use only one command to have `ls` display `atime`, `ctime`, and `mtime` at once. To do this, you need to create an alias that combines three commands by typing **alias dir="ls -l --time=ctime | grep root;ls -l | grep root;ls -l --time=atime | grep root"** and pressing **Enter**.

8. Type **dir** and press **Enter**. As shown in the following example, the first line of output shows the `ctime`, the second line shows the `mtime`, and the third line shows the `atime`:

```
-rw-r--r--    1    root    root    0    Oct 23    08:40    file1
-rw-r--r--    1    root    root    0    Oct 23    08:40    file1
-rw-r--r--    1    root    root    0    Oct 23    08:40    file1
```

9. Open the `file1` file. To see how the timestamps are affected, type **cat file1** and press **Enter**. (The file is empty, so there's no output from the `cat` command, but the `atime` is changed because the file was accessed.) Type **dir** and press **Enter**. Only the `atime` should have changed, as shown:

```
-rw-r--r--    1    root    root    0    Oct 23    08:40    file1
-rw-r--r--    1    root    root    0    Oct 23    08:40    file1
-rw-r--r--    1    root    root    0    Oct 23    08:47    file1
```

10. To modify the file with the vi editor, type **vi file1** and press **Enter**. Enter insert mode by typing **i**. To add file content, type **This is a test**. Press **Esc** to go back to command mode, and then type **:wq** and press **Enter**.

> You could simulate modifying the file by typing `touch file1` and pressing Enter.
>
> **TIP**

11. Type **dir** and press **Enter**. Notice that all three times have changed:

```
-rw-r--r--    1    root    root    0    Oct 23    08:50    file1
-rw-r--r--    1    root    root    0    Oct 23    08:50    file1
-rw-r--r--    1    root    root    0    Oct 23    08:50    file1
```

10

You probably expected mtime to change because you modified the file and atime to change because you had to access the file to modify it. However, ctime also changes, which might not make sense but that's how creation time values work in the Linux file system.

The result in Step 11 is different from other OSs, such as Windows. In these OSs, a file's creation time doesn't change just because its contents are modified.

12. If you change a file's permissions, do its timestamps change? If so, which of the three times changes? Type **chmod 700 file1** and press **Enter**, and then type **dir** and press **Enter**. You see that only the ctime changes:

```
-rwx   1   root   root   0   Oct 23   09:04   file1
-rwx   1   root   root   0   Oct 23   08:50   file1
-rwx   1   root   root   0   Oct 23   08:50   file1
```

13. What if you change a file's owners? Type **chown nobody file1** and press **Enter**, and then type **dir** and press **Enter**. Again, only the ctime changes. You get the same result if you change a file's attributes.

14. One attribute does affect time and date: The A attribute affects a file's atime. When this attribute is set, a file's atime isn't updated even though the file is accessed. To set this attribute, type **chattr +A file1** and press **Enter**. Then type **dir** and press **Enter** to see the current atime value. Access the file by using cat, and display the directory listing again with dir. You should see that the atime hasn't changed, despite accessing the file.

The A attribute is useful when you have frequently accessed files and you don't care about their atime values being updated. Using this attribute saves a little processing time and disk I/O.

15. As mentioned, you can change a file's timestamps with the touch command. When you use touch with no options, all three timestamps are updated. Type **touch file1** and press **Enter**, and then type **dir** and press **Enter** to see that all three times are the same.

16. The man page for the touch command states that the -a option specifies changing only the atime. Wait a minute or two, and then type **touch -a file1** and press **Enter**. Type **dir** and press **Enter**. As shown, both the atime and ctime values change:

```
-rwx   1   nobody   root   0   Oct 23   09:15   file1
-rwx   1   nobody   root   0   Oct 23   09:13   file1
-rwx   1   nobody   root   0   Oct 23   09:15   file1
```

17. Similarly, the -m option specifies changing only the mtime. Wait a minute or two, and then type **touch -m file1** and press **Enter**. Type **dir** and press **Enter**. Both the mtime and ctime values change.

Anything you do to a file, except open it and read from it, causes the ctime to change. Therefore, the ctime can be used only as an indication that something happened to change the file in some way.

18. You can use the atime to search for files that haven't been accessed recently. To find files that haven't been accessed in one year, for example, type **find / -atime 365** and press

Enter. The 365 is the number of days since the file was last accessed. Your Linux instal-lation is probably recent, so if the preceding command didn't return any files, try typing **find / -atime 7** and pressing **Enter.** (*Note*: Processing might take a while because the command is searching the entire file system.)

19. To use find to search for files based on their mtime values, type **find / -mtime 5** and press **Enter**, which searches for files that haven't been modified in five days.

You can also use the -exec or -ok options with the find com-mand to take some action, such as deleting or backing up, on files you've found, as you did in Lab 10.4.

TIP

20. Log out and shut down the system.

Review Questions

1. When you read a file's contents, which time is changed?

    a. ctime

    b. mtime

    c. atime

    d. All of the above

2. When you modify a file's contents, which time is changed?

    a. ctime

    b. mtime

    c. atime

    d. All of the above

3. Which time is changed when you use the command touch file9? (Choose all that apply.)

    a. ctime

    b. mtime

    c. atime

    d. None of the above

4. Which command displays mtime?

    a. ls -l

    b. ls -l -m

    c. ls -l --time=mtime

    d. ls -l --mtime

5. If you change a file's permissions with chmod, which time is changed?

    a. ctime

    b. mtime

    c. atime

    d. All of the above

10

C H A P T E R   11

COMPRESSION, SYSTEM BACKUP, AND SOFTWARE INSTALLATION

Labs included in this chapter

- Lab 11.1 Backing Up to a CD
- Lab 11.2 Compressing Programs with `gzexe`
- Lab 11.3 Compressing Image Files
- Lab 11.4 Installing and Removing Packages
- Lab 11.5 Detecting and Replacing Missing Package Files

CompTIA Linux+ Exam Objectives

Objective		Lab
104.3	Control mounting and unmounting of file systems	11.1
103.3	Perform basic file management	11.2, 11.3
102.5	Use RPM and YUM package management	11.5

Lab 11.1 Backing Up to a CD

Objectives

This lab explains how to burn data to a CD-R. In the first part, you convert your data into an ISO-9660 image that's compatible with CD media. In the second part, you use a CD burner program to place the image on a CD-R.

Materials Required

This lab requires the following:

- A computer running Fedora 13 Linux
- An IDE/ATAPI CD burner
- Two blank CD-Rs

Estimated completion time: 30 minutes

Activity

1. Start your Linux computer. Switch to a command-line terminal (`tty2`) by pressing **Ctrl+Alt+F2**, and log in as the root user.

2. Check to see whether your system recognizes its CD burner by typing **cdrecord -scanbus** and pressing **Enter**. You see quite a bit of output, ending with lines similar to the following:

```
scsibus1:
1,0,0100) 'ARTEC ' 'WRR-52Z ' '1.25' Removable CD-ROM
  *
  *
  *
  *
  *
  *
  *
```

The first line (`scsibus1:`) means that Linux sees this drive as a SCSI device, which is normal if you're using an IDE/ATAPI drive. The second line shows the drive manufacturer (ARTEC), the model number (WRR-52Z), and a description of the drive. Your information will likely be different.

 If your CD burner isn't in this list, you might not be able to do this lab.

3. You use the `genisoimage` command to create the ISO-9660 image that's burned to the CD-R. First, review the command's man page by typing **man genisoimage** and pressing **Enter**. When you have finished reading, press **q** to exit the man page.

4. Create an image of the `/etc` directory by typing **genisoimage -o /tmp/etc.iso -r /etc** and pressing **Enter**. As the program is running, you see a line similar to the following:

```
36.4% done, estimate finish Mon Sep 13 10:44:28 2012
```

You might see additional messages. When the process is finished, you see a summary of the data that's been written.

5. Type **ls -lh /tmp/etc.iso** and press **Enter**. You see output similar to the following, indicating that you've created an image that's about 31 MB:

```
-rw-r--r--  1  root  root  31M  Sep 13 15:32 /tmp/etc.iso
```

6. Before you burn the image to a CD-R, you should check whether the image was created according to your specifications. You can mount the image as though it were a CD. First, create the mount point by typing **mkdir /mnt/cdrom** and pressing **Enter**. Then type **mount -o loop /tmp/etc.iso /mnt/cdrom** and press **Enter** to mount the image.

7. Type **ls /mnt/cdrom** and press **Enter**. You should see the same files and directories that are in your /etc directory.

8. Insert a blank CD-R in the CD burner. Type **cdrecord speed=4 dev=/dev/cdrom /tmp/etc.iso** and press **Enter**. The cdrecord command displays a lot of text, and when the CD-R has finished being burned, you see a message similar to the following:

```
Track 01: Total bytes read/written: 31924224/31924224 (15588 sectors)
```

 The speed=4 parameter in Step 8 is a conservative value that should work with older and slower CD burners. Your CD burner might be capable of running at a higher speed.

9. To check whether the data was recorded to the CD-R, mount it by typing **mount -t iso9660 /dev/cdrom /mnt/cdrom** and pressing **Enter**. In this command, iso9660 is the file system type for the CD. You might see a message telling you that the device is write-protected, but that's okay because it's a CD. Now type **ls /mnt/cdrom** and press **Enter**. You should see the same files and directories that are in your /etc directory, and they should be the same as what you saw in the image file in Step 7.

10. Unmount the CD-R by typing **umount /dev/cdrom** and pressing **Enter**. Eject the CD-R by typing **eject /dev/cdrom** and pressing **Enter**.

11. If you have a computer running Windows, place the CD-R in its CD/DVD-ROM drive and look at the files on the CD-R. Notice that the filenames and directory names are in an 8.3 format (an uppercase name truncated to eight characters with a maximum three-character extension). You burned a CD-R that works with Linux but not with newer Windows versions.

12. If you want the Windows computer to see the same file and directory names as in Linux, configure genisoimage to use Microsoft Joliet (Unicode) names by typing **genisoimage -o /tmp/etc.iso -r -J /etc** and pressing **Enter**. The -r and -J options tell genisoimage how to format the file system. The old /tmp/etc.iso file is overwritten.

13. Place a blank CD-R in the CD burner and type **cdrecord speed=4 dev=/dev/cdrom /tmp/etc.iso** and press **Enter**. When the recording process is finished, eject the CD-R by typing **eject /dev/cdrom** and pressing **Enter**.

14. Place the CD-R in the Windows computer and examine the file and directory names. They should look the same as they do in Linux.

15. If you plan to continue to the next lab, stay logged in; otherwise, shut down the computer.

11

Review Questions

1. Which command is used to create ISO-9660 images?

   a. `cdrecord`

   b. `iso9660`

   c. `genisoimage`

   d. `mk9660`

2. Which command is used to write ISO-9660 images to a CD burner?

   a. `cdrecord`

   b. `iso9660`

   c. `genisoimage`

   d. `mk9660`

3. If you want Windows computers to see long file and directory names, what must you do when you have Linux burn a CD-R?

   a. Configure `cdrecord` for Rock Ridge extensions.

   b. Specify that `genisoimage` use Microsoft Joliet names.

   c. Make sure you load the NTFS kernel module.

   d. Specify the ISO-9660 format when you mount the image.

4. Which command indicates whether Linux recognizes your CD burner?

   a. `cdrecord devices`

   b. `mkisofs --devices`

   c. `cdrecord -scanbus`

   d. `lsdev -scan`

5. What's the command to mount an ISO image file named `backup.iso` in the `/home/back` directory to the `/media/myback` directory?

Lab 11.2 Compressing Programs with `gzexe`

Objectives

Making data files as small as possible is useful, particularly when they have to be stored on a small disk or must be transmitted over a slow network or modem link. Linux binary program files can be compressed for the same reasons. In this lab, you learn how to use the `gzexe` command to compress binary programs.

Materials Required

This lab requires the following:

- A computer running Fedora 13 Linux

Estimated completion time: 15 minutes

Activity

1. Switch to a command-line terminal (`tty2`) by pressing **Ctrl+Alt+F2,** and log in as the root user, if necessary.

2. Make sure you're in your home directory by typing **cd** and pressing **Enter.** Next, copy the `rpm` program from the `/bin` directory to your home directory by typing **cp /bin/rpm ./** and pressing **Enter.**

3. Find the `rpm` program's file size by typing **ls -l rpm** and pressing **Enter.** The file size should be about 22,452 bytes.

4. Compress the program by typing **gzexe rpm** and pressing **Enter.** This process takes a few seconds. When it's finished, you see a line similar to `rpm: 58%`. The number indicates the percentage of compression, so in this example, the `rpm` program was compressed by 58%.

5. The original file was renamed as `rpm~`, and the new compressed file is named `rpm`. Type **ls -l rpm*** and press **Enter** to see both file sizes. There should be a substantial difference, as shown:

```
-rwxr-xr-x  1  root  root  10222  10:22  rpm
-rwxr-xr-x  1  root  root  22452  10:21  rpm~
```

6. Both files still run the same program. Type **./rpm --version** and press **Enter.** You see output similar to `RPM version 4.8.0`, indicating the `rpm` program's version. Next, type **./rpm~ --version** and press **Enter.** You see that both the uncompressed file (`rpm~`) and the compressed file (`rpm`) work.

7. When you run the compressed program, it takes slightly longer to start because it must be uncompressed first. You can use the `time` command to compare the times both programs take to run. First, type **time ./rpm --version** and press **Enter** to see how long the compressed program takes to run. You see output similar to the following:

```
RPM version 4.8.0
real   0m0.024s
user   0m0.004s
sys    0m0.013s
```

The `time` command displays three results in a `minutes.seconds` format: the real elapsed time from program start to finish, the amount of time the program spent running as the user, and the amount of time the program spent running as the system.

8. Type **time ./rpm~ --version** and press **Enter** to see how long the uncompressed program takes to run. You should see that in all three results, it takes less time.

You can use the `-d` option with the `gzexe` command to return the compressed program to its original uncompressed state.

9. Delete the two `rpm` files you created by typing **rm rpm*** and pressing **Enter.** Press **y** and then **Enter** to confirm each deletion.

10. Log out and switch to the GUI if you're continuing to the next lab; otherwise, shut down the computer.

11

Review Questions

1. Which command compresses Linux binary programs and allows them to run in a compressed form?

   a. gzip

   b. compress

   c. gzexe

   d. rpm

2. When you issue the time cp /bin/rpm ./ command, what's the meaning of the output real 0m1.100s?

   a. The cp program ran for 1.1 minutes, using real-time priority.

   b. The cp program took 1.1 seconds to finish running.

   c. The rpm program took 1.1 seconds to finish running.

   d. The time program took 1 minute and 1 second to run the cp program.

3. A compressed binary program loads just as fast as the same uncompressed program. True or False?

4. The gzexe command enables you to convert a compressed program into its original uncompressed state. True or False?

5. What result does the time command display if a program takes 2 hours to run?

   a. 2h.0m0.000s

   b. 1h.60m0.000s

   c. 120m0.000s

   d. 2h.0m

Lab 11.3 Compressing Image Files

Objectives

In this lab, you use the cjpeg command to compress bitmap image files and convert them to JPEG format, which is useful for converting images to post on a Web page or send via e-mail or over the Internet. You can also use cjpeg to convert a JPEG image file from color to grayscale and compare the file size and image quality of compressed and uncompressed files.

Materials Required

This lab requires the following:

- A computer running Fedora 13 Linux
- A bitmap image (see steps for details)

Estimated completion time: 20 minutes

Activity

1. If necessary, log in to the GUI and open a terminal window.

2. This lab uses a bitmap image that should already be on your system, if you have OpenOffice installed. Type **cp /usr/lib/openoffice.org3/program/about.bmp ./** and press **Enter** to copy the about.bmp file to your home directory. To verify that the file was copied, type **ls -l *.bmp** and press **Enter**.

If you don't have OpenOffice, you can use `locate` to find another bitmap image. In Windows, you can capture bitmap images or create bitmap images in Paint. If you do this, name the file you capture or create about.bmp.

3. Some files have the file extension .bmp but aren't really bitmap image files. To check that a .bmp file is indeed a bitmap image, type **file about.bmp** and press **Enter**. If the file is a bitmap image, you see output similar to the following:

```
about.bmp: PC bitmap data, Windows 3.x format, 415 x 95 x 24
```

4. Next, you use cjpeg to convert the about.bmp file to a compressed .jpeg file. This command sends a compressed image to standard output, so you have to redirect it to a file by typing **cjpeg about.bmp > about.jpeg** and pressing **Enter**. Now you have a compressed image named about.jpeg.

5. Compare the .bmp and .jpeg file sizes by typing **ls -l about.*** and pressing **Enter**. The .jpeg file is much smaller than the .bmp file.

It's typical for a bitmap image file to compress to 15% to 20% of its original size.

6. To find out whether compressing the file affected its image quality, you need to look at both images in a graphics viewer program. Open your home folder by double-clicking the *user's* **Home folder** icon on your desktop (replacing *user* with the username you logged in with). Double-click **about.bmp** and then **about.jpeg**. The files open in separate windows. If you don't notice any difference in the images, that means you compressed the files without affecting the image quality much. Close the two windows displaying the files.

7. You can also use cjpeg to convert a color image to grayscale by using the -grayscale option. In the terminal window, type **cjpeg -grayscale about.bmp > about-gray.jpeg** and press **Enter**.

8. See how the grayscale image's file size compares with the other versions of the file by typing **ls -l about*** and pressing **Enter**. As shown, the grayscale .jpeg file is smaller than the full-color file:

```
-r--r--r--  1  root  root  118614  Aug 6  about.bmp
-rw-r--r--  1  root  root    5582  Aug 6  about-gray.jpeg
-rw-r--r--  1  root  root    7027  Aug 6  about.jpeg
```

9. Close all windows. If you plan to continue to the next lab, stay logged in; otherwise, shut down the computer.

11

Review Questions

1. Which command tells you whether a file with the `.bmp` extension is really a bitmap image?

   a. `ls -file`

   b. `bmp`

   c. `file`

   d. `ls -l * | grep bmp`

2. Which command can convert a bitmap image to a compressed image file?

   a. `file`

   b. `bmpcvt`

   c. `cjpeg`

   d. `jpeg`

3. If you convert a 100 KB bitmap file to a `.jpeg` file, the compressed file's approximate size is which of the following?

   a. 20 KB

   b. 120 KB

   c. 1.5 KB

   d. 15 MB

4. Write the command to convert a color bitmap image named `rainbow.bmp` to a grayscale JPEG file named `rainbow.jpeg`.

5. The `cjpeg` command enables you to compress a bitmap image and convert it to grayscale simultaneously. True or False?

Lab 11.4 Installing and Removing Packages

Objectives

Most Linux distributions use the Red Hat Package Manager (RPM) to install and uninstall software. In this lab, you learn how to do the following:

- Display all installed packages.
- Install packages from the Linux installation DVD.
- Uninstall packages.

Materials Required

This lab requires the following:

- A computer running Fedora 13 Linux
- Fedora 13 installation DVD

Estimated completion time: 15 minutes

Activity

1. Switch to a command-line terminal (`tty2`) by pressing **Ctrl+Alt+F2,** and log in as the root user.

2. To see a list of all packages installed on your computer, type **rpm -qa** and press **Enter.** Notice that they're not listed in alphabetic order. To sort them alphabetically and display them a page at a time, type **rpm -qa | sort | more** and press **Enter.** When you're finished reviewing the list, press **q** to quit `more`. To see whether a package named `cracklib` is installed, type **rpm -qa | grep cracklib** and press **Enter.** You should see three lines of output with the string `cracklib`. Use the same method to check for a package named `rdesktop`. You shouldn't see any output because the package isn't installed.

3. Insert the Fedora 13 DVD in the DVD-ROM drive, and then mount it by typing **mount -t iso9660 /dev/cdrom /mnt/cdrom** and pressing **Enter.** Switch to the `Packages` directory by typing **cd /mnt/cdrom/Packages** and pressing **Enter.**

 In Linux, package files aren't usually stored on the hard disk, as Windows `.cab` files are. You must mount the medium to install or reinstall a package.

4. Find the `rdesktop` package's full name by typing **ls rdesk*** and pressing **Enter.** In Fedora 13, it's `rdesktop-1.6.0-7.fc12.i686.rpm`.

5. Install the `rdesktop` package by typing **rpm -i rdesk*** and pressing **Enter.** You can use wildcards instead of typing the entire name as long as there are no name conflicts. (You can also use the Tab key completion feature described in Chapter 3 of the accompanying textbook.)

6. To verify that the `rdesktop` package is installed, type **rpm -qp rdesk*** and press **Enter.** (The `q` option means query, and the `p` option allows using wildcards to find a package name.) You should see the following line:

   ```
   rdesktop-1.6.0-7.fc12.i686
   ```

7. Get information about the package by typing **rpm -qi rdesktop-1.6.0-7.fc12.i686** and pressing **Enter.** Unfortunately, you can't use wildcards in this command. A lot of text describing the package is displayed.

8. Use another method of verifying that the package was installed by typing **whereis rdesktop** and pressing **Enter.** You see the following:

   ```
   rdesktop: /usr/bin/rdesktop /usr/share/rdesktop
    /usr/share/man/man1/rdesktop.1.gz
   ```

9. Next, uninstall the package with the `-e` (erase) option by typing **rpm -e rdesktop-1.6.0-7.fc12.i686** and pressing **Enter.** (You can't use a wildcard to uninstall a package.) If the uninstall is successful, nothing is displayed onscreen.

10. Verify that the package was uninstalled by typing **whereis rdesktop** and pressing **Enter.** You should see `rdesktop:`, which means the package can't be found.

11. Remove the DVD by typing **cd;umount /dev/cdrom;eject** and pressing **Enter.**

12. If you plan to continue to the next lab, stay logged in; otherwise, shut down the computer.

11

Review Questions

1. Which command displays all packages installed on your computer?

   a. `rpm --list`

   b. `rpm -q`

   c. `rpm -qa`

   d. `rpm -q all`

2. Which command displays the names of all installed packages starting with x?

   a. `rpm -q x*`

   b. `rpm -qa x*`

   c. `rpm -qp x*`

   d. `rpm -qa | grep x`

3. Which command installs the `blivet-2.3` package if the `rpm` file in the current directory is `blivet-2.3.rpm`?

   a. `rpm -i blivet`

   b. `rpm -a blivet-2.3`

   c. `rpm -i blivet*`

   d. `rpm -a blivet-2.3.rpm`

4. Which command uninstalls the `blivet-2.3` package if the `rpm` file on the installation DVD is `blivet-2.3.rpm`?

   a. `rpm -u blivet*`

   b. `rpm -u blivet-2.3`

   c. `rpm -e blivet-2.3`

   d. `rpm -e blivet*`

5. To check whether a package is installed, you can use the `locate` command immediately after using `rpm`. True or False?

Lab 11.5 Detecting and Replacing Missing Package Files

Objectives

Sometimes files are erased from a hard disk because of a user mistake or an attack. If these files are part of a package, the programs in the package might not run or might not run correctly. You need some way to detect when files are missing and a means to replace them. Package managers can do that for you. This lab shows you how the Red Hat Package Manager (RPM) performs these functions.

Materials Required

This lab requires the following:

- A computer running Fedora 13 Linux
- Fedora 13 installation DVD

Estimated completion time: 20 minutes

Activity

1. Switch to a command-line terminal (`tty2`) by pressing **Ctrl+Alt+F2**, and log in as the root user, if necessary.

2. The `gzip` package is installed on most Linux computers. To find its package name, type **rpm -qa | grep gzip** and press **Enter**. It's probably named `gzip-1.3.13-3.fc13.i686`.

3. To get a package description by using the `-i` option, type **rpm -qi gzip-1.3.13-3.fc13.i686** and press **Enter**.

4. To see what files are part of the package by using the `-l` option, type **rpm -ql gzip-1.3.13-3.fc13.i686** and press **Enter**.

 The `-l` option shows you files that are part of a package. It doesn't necessarily show you the files installed on the hard disk.

5. To see whether all files that are part of the package are actually installed on the hard disk, use the `-V` option by typing **rpm -V gzip-1.3.13-3.fc13.i686** and pressing **Enter**. If all the files are on the hard disk, there's no output from the `rpm` program.

6. Delete some of these files by typing **rm /usr/share/man/man1/gzip*** and pressing **Enter**. Press **y** and **Enter** if you're prompted to confirm the file deletion.

7. To see how `rpm` handles the missing files, type **rpm -V gzip-1.3.13-3.fc13.i686** and press **Enter**. You should see output similar to this:

```
missing d /usr/share/man/man1/gzip.1.gz
```

8. To fix the problem, you need to reinstall the files from the DVD. Insert the Fedora 13 DVD in the DVD-ROM drive. Mount it by typing **mount -t iso9660 /dev/cdrom /mnt/cdrom** and pressing **Enter**, and then go to the `Packages` directory on the DVD.

9. Install the missing files (the ones deleted in Step 6) by typing **rpm -i --replacepkgs gzip-1.3.13-3.fc13.i686.rpm** and pressing **Enter**.

10. To check again whether all package files are installed, type **rpm -V gzip-1.3.13-3.fc13.i686** and press **Enter**. Nothing's displayed because no files are missing.

11. In previous steps, you checked whether any files in a package were missing from the hard disk. To check whether there are any missing files for all packages installed on your system, type **rpm -Va** and press **Enter**. This process takes a while.

12. Remove the DVD by typing **cd;umount /dev/cdrom;eject** and pressing **Enter**, and then shut down the computer.

11

Review Questions

1. Which command displays information about the words-2-17 package?

   a. rpm -i words-2-17

   b. rpm -qa words-2-17

   c. rpm -iq words-2-17

   d. rpm -qi words-2-17

2. Which command shows you the files that are part of a package?

   a. rpm -q words-2-17

   b. rpm -qa words-2-17

   c. rpm -ql words-2-17

   d. rpm -qi words-2-17

3. Which command shows you files that are part of a package but not installed on the hard disk?

   a. rpm -q words-2-17

   b. rpm -ql words-2-17

   c. rpm -V words-2-17

   d. rpm -Z words-2-17

4. RPM package files are usually stored on the hard disk, similar to Windows .cab files. True or False?

5. The rpm -i -fixfiles words-2-17 command can fix the words-2-17 package if some of its files are missing. True or False?

NETWORK CONFIGURATION

Labs included in this chapter

- Lab 12.1 Configuring Ethernet Interfaces
- Lab 12.2 Creating IP Aliases
- Lab 12.3 Installing and Configuring NcFTPd
- Lab 12.4 Using Advanced Options with Network Tools

CompTIA Linux+ Exam Objectives

Objective		Lab
109.1	Fundamentals of Internet protocols	12.1–12.4
109.2	Basic network configuration	12.1–12.3
109.3	Basic network troubleshooting	12.4

Lab 12.1 Configuring Ethernet Interfaces

Objectives

This lab shows you how to change any interface parameter in real time without having to restart Linux. In particular, it shows you how to change an Ethernet NIC's IP address, subnet mask, broadcast address, and MAC address. You also learn how to set the default route for packets going outside a local network segment.

Materials Required

This lab requires the following:

- A computer running Fedora 13 Linux
- A LAN connection

Estimated completion time: 15 minutes

Activity Background

The main command you use when dealing with interfaces and IP addresses is `ifconfig` (which stands for "interface configuration"). In this lab, you configure an Ethernet NIC. The first Ethernet NIC on a machine is called `eth0` by default. If you have a second Ethernet card, it's called `eth1`.

The Windows version of `ifconfig` is `ipconfig`. Both commands perform similar functions, but `ifconfig` has more capabilities for configuring a network interface. Window's `ipconfig` is used mainly to display IP configuration information.

You also learn to use the `route` command to set the default gateway, which is the router acting as a default exit point for communication to networks outside a local network segment.

Activity

1. Start your Linux computer. Switch to a command-line terminal (`tty2`) by pressing **Ctrl+Alt+F2**, and log in as the root user.

2. Issuing `ifconfig` with no parameters displays a status message for all interfaces. Type **ifconfig** and press **Enter**. You should see output similar to the following when the only interface is a single Ethernet NIC (`eth0`):

```
eth0  Link encap:Ethernet HWaddr 00:07:95:BB:A3:6A
    inet addr:192.168.0.1 Bcast:192.168.0.255 Mask:255.255.255.0
    inet6 addr: fe80::20c:29ff:fe79:140f/64 Scope: Link
    UP BROADCAST RUNNING MULTICAST MTU:1500 Metric:1 RX
    ...
    lo  Link encap:Local Loopback
inet addr:127.0.0.1 Mask:255.0.0.0
...
```

The `lo` in the preceding output refers to the local loopback network device, which you learn more about in Lab 12.2.

3. To change a NIC's IP address, you pass the new address as a parameter by typing **ifconfig eth0 192.168.0.2** and pressing **Enter**.

4. To view an interface's status, specify its name by typing **ifconfig eth0** and pressing **Enter**. You see output similar to what's shown in Step 2, but no information about `lo` is displayed.

5. To change the subnet mask, type **ifconfig eth0 netmask 255.255.255.240** and press **Enter**.

6. Again, display `eth0`'s status. You should see that the `Mask` value has changed.

7. To display only the lines showing the IP address (`inet addr`), broadcast address (`Bcast`), and subnet mask (`Mask`) as well as IPv6 address information (`inet6`), type **ifconfig eth0 | grep inet** and press **Enter**. You see output similar to the following:

```
inet addr:192.168.0.2 Bcast:192.168.0.15 Mask:255.255.255.240
inet6 addr: fe80::20c:29ff:fe79:140f/64 Scope: Link
```

8. Sometimes you need to change an Ethernet NIC's MAC address if, for example, your company uses locally administered MAC addresses. In Step 2, the MAC address is 00:07:95:BB:A3:6A. You can change it, but you must shut down the interface first by typing **ifconfig eth0 down** and pressing **Enter**.

While an interface is down, your computer can't send or receive packets on it.

9. Change the MAC address by typing **ifconfig eth0 hw ether 00:00:0B:AD:F0:0D** and pressing **Enter**.

10. Restart the interface by typing **ifconfig eth0 up** and pressing **Enter**. Verify that the MAC address has changed by typing **ifconfig eth0 | grep eth0** and pressing **Enter**. You should see the following:

```
eth0 Link encap:Ethernet HWaddr 00:00:0B:AD:F0:0D
```

11. The `ifconfig` command can't be used to configure one important parameter: the default route (default gateway). You must use the `route` command to set it. If you issue `route` without command-line options, it displays the routing table. However, it tries to resolve IP addresses in the table to names by using DNS. To disable DNS lookups, you use the `-n` option by typing **route -n** and pressing **Enter**. The routing table should be similar to this example:

```
Kernel IP routing table
Destination Gateway Genmask       Flags  Metric  Ref Use  Iface
192.168.0.0 0.0.0.0 255.255.255.240 U      0       0   0    eth0
```

12

The Linux internal router uses a routing table to determine where packets need to be sent so that they arrive at their destinations. The `route` command is also useful for troubleshooting network problems.

If the `eth0` interface is using DHCP for IP address assignment, the process of shutting down the interface and restarting it resets the interface to use DHCP, thus overriding the address and subnet mask you set previously. In this case, ask your instructor what address to use in Step 12 when you set the default gateway.

12. To add a default gateway for a router or device with the IP address 192.168.0.14, type **route add default gw 192.168.0.14** and press **Enter**. See how your routing table was affected by typing **route -n** again and pressing **Enter**. There should be an entry for the new gateway, as shown in the following example:

```
Kernel IP routing table
Destination   Gateway        Genmask          Flags Metric  Ref Use Iface
192.168.0.0   0.0.0.0        255.255.255.240 U     0       0   0   eth0
0.0.0.0       192.168.0.14   0.0.0.0          UG    0       0   0   eth0
```

13. Leave your computer in its current configuration to continue to Lab 12.2.

Review Questions

1. What's the name of the first Ethernet interface?

   a. `eth0`

   b. `eth1`

   c. `etha`

   d. `eth0:0`

2. Which Linux command is used to change the subnet mask?

   a. `netmask`

   b. `ifconfig`

   c. `ipconfig`

   d. `route`

3. An Ethernet card's MAC address can be changed with the `route` command. True or False?

4. To change an interface's MAC address, you must shut down the interface first. True or False?

5. Which command is used to set the default gateway?

   a. `netmask`

   b. `ifconfig`

   c. `ipconfig`

   d. `route`

Lab 12.2 Creating IP Aliases

Objectives

Lab 12.1 showed you how to use basic `ifconfig` functions, such as setting an Ethernet NIC's IP address, subnet mask, and broadcast address. This lab covers a more advanced use, creating IP aliases (assigning more than one IP address to a single physical interface). You also examine in more detail the status information `ifconfig` displays.

Materials Required

This lab requires the following:

- A computer running Fedora 13 Linux
- A LAN connection
- Your computer in its state at the end of Lab 12.1

Estimated completion time: 15 minutes

Activity Background

Each physical interface can have more than one IP address assigned. When you assign another IP address to a physical interface, you're creating an IP alias. You can create up to 256 IP aliases for each physical interface and even assign IP aliases to the local loopback interface. The local loopback (`lo`) interface is a special logical device (meaning it doesn't exist physically) used to move network packets in a single host. It can be useful in testing networking functions without needing network access to another computer. Creating IP aliases for the local loopback interface can also be helpful in advanced networking applications, such as building a Web server.

Activity

1. You should already be logged in to `tty2` as root. If not, switch to `tty2`, and log in as the root user.

2. To create an IP alias, you must base its name on the physical interface's name. The first Ethernet NIC is called `eth0` by default, so create an IP alias called `eth0:0` by typing **ifconfig eth0:0 1.1.1.1** and pressing **Enter**.

 These steps show you how to create IP aliases. The actual IP addresses you use depend on your network.

12

3. To view the new alias, you issue `ifconfig` with no parameters, so type **ifconfig** and press **Enter**. You see output similar to the following:

```
eth0   Link encap:Ethernet HWaddr 00:07:95:BB:A3:6A
   inet addr:192.168.0.1 Bcast:192.168.0.255 Mask:255.255.255.0
   inet6 addr: fe80::20c:29ff:fe79:140f/64 Scope: Link
   UP BROADCAST RUNNING MULTICAST MTU:1500 Metric:1 RX
...
```

```
eth0:0  Link encap:Ethernet HWaddr 00:07:95:BB:A3:6A
inet addr:1.1.1.1 Bcast:1.255.255.255 Mask:255.0.0.0
...
lo  Link encap:Local Loopback
inet addr:127.0.0.1 Mask:255.0.0.0
...
```

4. Next, create another IP alias by typing **ifconfig eth0:5 1.2.3.4** and pressing **Enter**. You should have two IP aliases. Use `ifconfig` again to verify the new alias.

5. Type **ifconfig eth0:5** and press **Enter** to view information about only `eth0:5`.

6. The convention is to use numbers following the interface name (`eth`) and colons for IP aliases, but you can use anything you like. Type **ifconfig eth0:abc 1.2.3.5** and press **Enter**, and then type **ifconfig eth0:abc** and press **Enter** to see the new alias.

7. Now create two IP aliases for the local loopback (`lo`) interface by typing **ifconfig lo:0 127.0.0.2** and pressing **Enter**, and then typing **ifconfig lo:1 127.0.0.3** and pressing **Enter**. Type **ifconfig | more** and press **Enter** to see all the interfaces you've created so far.

8. To shut down an IP alias, type **ifconfig eth0:5 down** and press **Enter**, and then type **ifconfig | more** and press **Enter** to see that the `eth0:5` interface is no longer listed.

9. If you try to restart an IP alias that's been shut down, you can't. You must re-create it. To see how it works, try restarting the alias by typing **ifconfig eth0:5 up** and pressing **Enter**. You get the following error message:

```
SIOCSIFFLAGS: Cannot assign requested address
```

10. To communicate with the alias, type **ping 1.1.1.1** and press **Enter**. You see the `ping` reply messages. The `ping` command continues sending packets to the destination IP address until you press Ctrl+C. Press **Ctrl+C** now.

11. The changes you made to interfaces and IP settings are in effect only until you restart the computer, when the settings are initialized according to the interface's configuration file (`/etc/sysconfig/network-scripts/ifcfg-eth0`). Restart the computer if you're continuing to the next lab; otherwise, shut it down.

Review Questions

1. Which command configures an IP alias?

   a. `ifconfig -alias 192.168.0.50`

   b. `ifconfig eth0-alias 192.168.0.50`

   c. `ifconfig eth0:0 192.168.0.50`

   d. `ifconfig eth0:0 192.168.0.50 -a`

2. You can't assign IP aliases to the local loopback (`lo`) interface. True or False?

3. How many IP aliases can be created?

   a. Up to 64 per physical interface

   b. Up to 256 per physical interface

   c. Up to 64, regardless of the number of physical interfaces

   d. Up to 256, regardless of the number of physical interfaces

4. When you shut down a physical interface, you must specify the IP address, subnet mask, and broadcast address again when you restart the interface. True or False?

5. An IP alias is used only for internal testing; you can't actually send packets to the IP address assigned to the alias and get a response. True or False?

Lab 12.3 Installing and Configuring NcFTPd

Objectives

FTP is a common method of transferring files over a network. One widely used FTP server for Linux is WuFTP, included in nearly all Linux distributions. However, it can be difficult to configure and has had security vulnerabilities. Experienced Linux users and administrators often use other FTP server software, such as NcFTPd. In this lab, you download, install, and configure NcFTPd.

Materials Required

This lab requires the following:

- A computer running Fedora 13 Linux
- A Web browser and access to the Internet

Estimated completion time: 45 minutes

Activity

1. Start your computer, if necessary, and log in to the GUI as a regular user. Start a Web browser and go to **www.ncftp.com/ncftpd**.

2. Read the home page to learn the benefits of using this FTP server. Note that NcFTPd doesn't use `inetd` or `xinetd`, which improves performance, and doesn't have to call other programs, such as `/bin/ls`, to do its job.

3. Click the **security** link to learn why NcFTPd is more secure than WuFTP. Go back to the home page, and click the **Download Now!** link.

4. Next, you choose the software version for your computer and OS; this lab assumes you're running Linux on an Intel-based computer. Click the **NcFTPd Server X.X.X for Linux (Intel YY-bit)** link (replacing X.X.X with the version and YY with 32 or 64). Most likely, you should download the 32-bit version, but if you aren't sure, ask your instructor.

5. You're downloading a compressed file (tarball). By default, this file is saved in the `Downloads` subdirectory of your home directory. Switch to the second virtual console (`tty2`), and log in with the same username you used to log in to the GUI.

6. Switch to the `Downloads` subdirectory by typing **cd Downloads** and pressing **Enter**. Uncompress the file by typing **tar xzvf ncftpd** and pressing **Tab** to fill out the rest of the long filename. Press **Enter** to start the `tar` program.

7. To go to the new subdirectory you created, type **cd ncftpd**, press **Tab** to fill out the rest of the directory name, and then press **Enter**.

12

8. To install the software, switch to the root user by typing **su** and pressing **Enter**, and then type the root password and press **Enter**. Type **./install_ncftpd.pl** and press **Enter**. You see output similar to the following:

```
Created /etc/ftpusers
Using /var/ftp for ftp-home
No FTP server is running.
...
CONGRATULATIONS! NcFTPd has been successfully installed. Your
next step is to customize your installation by editing:
/usr/local/etc/ncftpd/general.cf
/usr/local/etc/ncftpd/domain.cf
...
```

9. To verify that NcFTPd is running, display its processes by typing **ps ax | grep ncftpd** and pressing **Enter**. You see several lines of output showing processes related to NcFTPd.

10. Type **ps aux | grep ncftpd** and press **Enter**. Notice that all the NcFTPd processes are running as the root user. The u option in this command specifies displaying the user who started the process.

11. When an ordinary user logs in to the FTP server, the working directory is set to the user's home directory. When an anonymous user logs in, the working directory is set to /var/ftp. To place a file in this directory so that you can tell when you're in it, type **touch /var/ftp/file1** and press **Enter**. Type **ls -l /var/ftp/file1** and press **Enter** to verify that the file is owned by the root user and group.

12. Type **exit** and press **Enter** to switch back to the user you logged in as originally, and then type **cd** and press **Enter** to go to your home directory. Next, you create a file with an unusual name so that you can recognize it easily when you log in to the FTP server as this user later. To do this, type **touch crazyfile** and press **Enter**.

13. Connect to the FTP server by typing **ftp localhost** and pressing **Enter**. You see output similar to the following:

```
Connected to localhost (127.0.0.1).
220 fedora13.localdomain NcFTPd Server (unregistered copy) ready.
Name (localhost:username):
```

14. To log in as an anonymous user, type **anonymous** and press **Enter**. You see the following:

```
331 Guest login ok, send your complete e-mail address
as password.
Password:
```

15. Type whatever e-mail address you like and press **Enter**. You see this output:

```
230-You are user #1 of 50 simultaneous users allowed.
230-
230 Logged in anonymously.
Remote system type is UNIX.
Using binary mode to transfer files.
ftp>
```

By default, NcFTPd requires logging in within 15 seconds. If you don't, you see an error message and an `ftp>` prompt. You can log in again by entering `open localhost`.

16. Because you logged in as an anonymous user, the directory should be `/var/ftp`. To see whether this is true, type **ls** and press **Enter**. You see the `file1` file you created in the `/var/ftp` directory in Step 11, but the owner is now `ftpuser` because the NcFTPd server hides the file's real owner from FTP clients. You also see a `README` file.

17. Type **?** and press **Enter** to see a list of available commands.

18. To transfer the `README` file to your working directory, type **get README** and press **Enter**. Type **! cat README** and press **Enter** to view the file's contents. The `!` command tells the FTP server you want to run a command from the shell.

19. Disconnect from the FTP server but don't exit the FTP client by typing **close** and pressing **Enter**. You see this message:

    ```
    221 Goodbye.
    ftp>
    ```

20. Connect to the FTP server by typing **open localhost** and pressing **Enter**. When you're prompted for your username, type the username for your regular user account, and then enter your password.

21. Because you logged in as an ordinary user, you should be in that user account's home directory. To verify, type **ls** and press **Enter**. You see the `crazyfile` file you created in Step 12.

22. Exit `ftp` by typing **quit** and pressing **Enter**, and then log out of `tty2`. Keep the computer running if you're continuing to the next lab; otherwise, shut down the computer.

Review Questions

1. Which of the following reasons explains why NcFTPd performs better than WuFTP?

   a. It doesn't spawn child processes when users connect.

   b. It uses `/bin/ls`.

   c. It uses a different transport protocol from other FTP programs.

   d. It doesn't do directory caching.

2. When a user logs in as an ordinary (nonanonymous) user, the working directory is `/var/ftp`. True or False?

3. When a user logs in as anonymous, the working directory is `/ftp/anonymous`. True or False?

4. What command do you use to disconnect from the FTP server but not exit the FTP client?

   a. `disconnect`

   b. `exit`

   c. `quit`

   d. `close`

5. When anonymous users look at a listing of files in the default FTP directory, the owner is always `ftpuser`. True or False?

12

Lab 12.4 Using Advanced Options with Network Tools

Objectives

You have used the basic options in `ifconfig`, `ping`, and `traceroute`. In this lab, you use more advanced options with these command-line tools.

Materials Required

This lab requires the following:

- A computer running Fedora 13 Linux
- An Internet connection

Estimated completion time: 30 minutes

Activity

1. Switch to `tty2`, and log in as the root user.

2. Type **man ifconfig** and press **Enter** to view the man pages, and scroll down to the Options section. Notice that you can configure an interface to enable and disable certain types of traffic by using the `arp/-arp`, `promisc/-promisc`, and `allmulti/-allmulti` options. (You experiment with the `arp/-arp` options in this lab.) When you're finished, press **q** to quit the man pages.

3. Type **route** and press **Enter** to get your default gateway's IP address. To find the default gateway's MAC address, type **ping** *default-gateway* and press **Enter** (replacing *default-gateway* with the IP address you found with the `route` command). Press **Ctrl+C** to stop the `ping` command.

4. You might be familiar with using the `arp` command in Windows to display the ARP table. In Fedora 13 Linux, you use the `ip neighbor` command. Type **ip neighbor** and press **Enter**. You see output similar to the following:

   ```
   172.31.250 dev eth0 lladdr 00:0f:34:e5:63:b0 REACHABLE
   ```

   The last part of the output might be different from REACHABLE, depending on how long you took to type `ip neighbor` after issuing the `ping` command. However, the output shows that your computer has the default gateway's MAC address.

5. Type **ifconfig eth0 -arp** and press **Enter** to disable ARP on the `eth0` interface. Now the `eth0` interface can neither receive nor send ARP packets.

6. Wait a couple of minutes so that your computer doesn't access the network, and then type **ip neighbor** and press **Enter**. By now, the default gateway's entry should have expired, and you see output similar to the following:

   ```
   172.31.1.250 dev eth0 FAILED
   ```

   If you still see an entry for the default gateway that includes the MAC address, continue entering the `ip neighbor` command periodically until you see output similar to the preceding line.

7. Ping the default gateway as you did in Step 3. You should see a message similar to From 172.31.1.20 icmp_seq=1 Destination Host Unreachable because your computer couldn't access the default gateway's MAC address and, therefore, couldn't communicate with it. The IP protocol depends on ARP to resolve IP addresses to MAC addresses.

8. To enable ARP again, type **ifconfig eth0 arp** and press **Enter**. Try to ping the default gateway again to verify that you can. Press **Ctrl+C** to exit.

9. Type **man ping** and press **Enter** to view the man pages. You use the -s, -t, -c, and -M options in this lab, so read about these options. When you're finished, press **q** to quit the man pages.

10. Type **ping -c 5 www.google.com** and press **Enter** to send five ping messages of 64 bytes each (the default size of a ping message) to *www.google.com*. Note the time values. Next, type **ping -c 5 -s 5000 www.google.com** and press **Enter** to send five ping messages of 5000 bytes each. The times increase by a few milliseconds per packet.

11. Type **ping -c 5 -t 20 www.google.com** and press **Enter** to send five ping messages with the time-to-live (TTL) value 20 specified by the -t option. The TTL value specifies how many routers the ping message can traverse before it times out. A TTL of 20 should get the packet to the site no matter where you are. Next, type **ping -c 5 -t 2 www.google.com** and press **Enter**. You probably get the message Time to live exceeded because the packet needs to traverse more than two routers to get to *www.google.com*. Continue to send ping packets to *www.google.com*, increasing the value in the -t option each time until you get replies. The value needed for the -t option to get replies is the number of routers the packets have to go through to get to *www.google.com*.

The ping reply indicates a TTL value (such as ttl=55 in the output). If you know the starting TTL value in the reply packet *www.google. com* sends, you can determine the number of routers by subtracting the starting TTL value from the reply's TTL value. The starting TTL value of ping packets in most Linux OSs is 64, and in Windows, it's 128.

12. IP packet fragmentation slows down networks and can cause reliability problems. By default, IP fragments packets if they're too large for the maximum transmission unit (MTU). To determine the maximum packet size that can be sent to a destination without fragmentation, you use the -M option by typing **ping -M do -c 5 -s 1472 www.google.com** and pressing **Enter**. The ping should go through successfully. Next, type **ping -M do -c 5 -s 1473 www.google.com** and press **Enter**. You probably get the message Frag needed and DF set (mtu=1500).

The -M do option tells ping not to fragment messages, so the DF (do not fragment) flag in the packet header is set. The second ping command set the size to 1473, which, along with the headers, exceeds the MTU of 1500 bytes.

13. Type **man traceroute** and press **Enter** to see the man pages, and review the available options. (You use the -f option in this lab, so make sure you read about it.) Press **q** to quit the man pages.

12

14. Type **traceroute -f 1 www.google.com** and press **Enter**. The -f option specifies the starting TTL; this first test uses the default value, which is 1. Notice that the trace starts with the default gateway router. To get trace information starting with the fifth router in the path, type **traceroute -f 5 www.google.com** and press **Enter**. Experiment with other options, such as -T (which uses TCP instead of ICMP as the probing protocol).

15. Log out and shut down your computer.

Review Questions

1. What command do you use to see the contents of the ARP cache?

   a. `ifconfig -arp`

   b. `ip neighbor`

   c. `arp -d`

   d. `ping -a`

2. What's the consequence of disabling ARP on an interface?

   a. ARP packets can be sent but not received.

   b. The interface can no longer resolve names to IP addresses.

   c. The interface can no longer find MAC addresses.

   d. The interface's communication speed increases.

3. Which `ping` option prevents transmitting very large packets?

   a. `-s 2000`

   b. `-M do`

   c. `-c DF`

   d. `-t 1500`

4. By default, IP packets that exceed the MTU aren't fragmented. True or False?

5. Which command uses TCP and starts reporting trace information at the third router?

   a. `traceroute -T -f 3`

   b. `ping /TCP -3`

   c. `traceroute -T 3 -f`

   d. `ping -R 3 /T`

CONFIGURING NETWORK SERVICES

Labs included in this chapter

- Lab 13.1 Installing and Configuring a Telnet Server
- Lab 13.2 Installing and Configuring NIS
- Lab 13.3 Working with the Firewall

CompTIA Linux+ Exam Objectives

Objective		Lab
109.2	Basic network configuration	13.1, 13.2
110.1	Perform security administration tasks	13.3

Lab 13.1 Installing and Configuring a Telnet Server

Objectives

The goal of this lab is to learn how to install a Telnet server and connect to it. In addition, you learn to use yum, a package manager that attempts to download a requested package from the Internet.

Materials Required

This lab requires the following:

- A computer running Fedora 13 Linux
- An Internet connection

Estimated completion time: 15 minutes

Activity Background

Although Telnet isn't a secure method of establishing a communication with a Linux computer, you might need to have it available in case your client computer doesn't have the SSH client installed, for example.

Activity

1. Start your Linux computer, log in to the GUI, and then open a terminal window. To switch to the root user, type **su** and press **Enter**, and then enter the root password.

2. Type **yum install telnet-server** and press **Enter**. If the package has to be downloaded, you get the following message:

```
Total download size 157 k
Installed size: 307 k
Is this ok [y/N]:
```

3. Type **y** and press **Enter** to download and install the package. To view the Telnet configuration file, /etc/xinetd.d/telnet, that's created, type **cat /etc/xinetd.d/telnet** and press **Enter**. The file looks like the following:

```
# default: on
# description: The telnet server serves telnet sessions; it uses
# unencrypted username/password pairs for authentication.
service telnet
{
  flags = REUSE
  socket_type = stream
  wait = no
  user = root
  server = /usr/sbin/in.telnetd
  log_on_failure +=USERID
  disable = yes
}
```

4. As you can see in the last line, the Telnet server is disabled by default. Enable it by typing **chkconfig telnet on** and pressing **Enter**. To view the Telnet configuration file again, type

cat /etc/xinetd.d/telnet and press **Enter**. The `disable` = yes line has been changed to `disable` = no and moved to the first line.

5. Next, start or restart the `xinetd` daemon by typing **service xinetd restart** and pressing **Enter**. You might get a "Failed" message when stopping the service if it wasn't running, but, you should get an "OK" message when the service is started.

6. To test the Telnet server, type **telnet localhost** and press **Enter**. When prompted, log in as an ordinary user.

The root user is prohibited from logging in through Telnet.

TIP

7. Type **exit** and press **Enter** to close the Telnet connection.

8. By default, the firewall blocks Telnet connections, but it doesn't block these connections when you start them from the local computer. To allow Telnet connections from a remote computer, click **System**, point to **Administration**, and click **Firewall**. Click **Close** in the Firewall Configuration Startup message box.

9. When prompted to authenticate as the root user, type the root password and click **Authenticate**.

10. The Firewall Configuration dialog box opens to the Trusted Services pane (see Figure 13-1). A number of services are listed that you can configure as trusted; however, because Telnet isn't a secure protocol, it's not listed. Click **Other Ports** on the left.

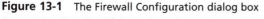

Figure 13-1 The Firewall Configuration dialog box

Source: Fedora Linux (http://fedoraproject.org)

13

11. Next, you open the port for connecting to the Telnet server. Click **Add**. In the Port and Protocol dialog box, scroll down and click the **23 TCP telnet** line, and then click **OK**. Click **Apply**, and then click **Yes**. If prompted, type the root password and click **Authenticate**. Close the Firewall Configuration dialog box.

12. If you have another computer with the Telnet client installed, test the connection, and then exit.

13. Close all open windows. If you're continuing to the next lab, stay logged in; otherwise, shut down the computer.

Review Questions

1. Which command installs the Telnet server package with the `yum` package manager?

    a. `rpm -install telnet-server`

    b. `yum --install telnet`

    c. `yum install telnet-server`

    d. `rpm install telnet`

2. Which of the following is true about the Telnet server in Fedora 13 Linux?

    a. It's disabled by default.

    b. After it's enabled, you can immediately connect remotely.

    c. You can't log in as an ordinary user; you can log in only as root.

    d. The connection is encrypted.

3. You have just installed the `telnet-server` package and tested it by logging in from the local computer. Are there any additional steps to take before you can log in remotely?

    a. There are no additional steps.

    b. Enable UDP port 13 on the firewall.

    c. Configure encryption for the Telnet protocol.

    d. Enable TCP port 23 on the firewall.

4. Telnet is a good choice when you need a secure remote terminal session. True or False?

5. By default, a Telnet server is installed and ready to use in Fedora 13 Linux. True or False?

Lab 13.2 Installing and Configuring NIS

Objectives

The goal of this lab is to learn how to configure a Network Information Service (NIS) server. Configuring the client requires two Linux servers, so you don't do this task in this lab. If you have a second Linux computer, you can go through the client configuration process (explained in Chapter 13 of the accompanying textbook).

Materials Required

This lab requires the following:

- A computer running Fedora 13 Linux
- An Internet connection

Estimated completion time: 15 minutes

Activity

1. If necessary, start your Linux computer, switch to a command-line terminal, and log in to the terminal as root.

2. Type **yum install ypserv** and press **Enter**. When you see the prompt Is this ok [y/N], press **y** and then **Enter**. You see the message Complete! when the installation is finished.

3. Type **domainname F13_domain** (or substitute another name for F13_domain) and press **Enter**.

4. To make the domain name permanent, open the /etc/sysconfig/network file in a text editor, and add the line **NISDOMAIN="F13_domain"** at the end of the file. Save and close the file.

5. Next, open the /var/yp/Makefile file in a text editor, navigate to the line beginning with **all:**, and then delete the word **mail** in that line. Save and close the file.

6. In a text editor, create a new file named /var/yp/securenets. If you don't create this file, any computer can share your user and password information. Add a line listing your network's subnet mask and network address. For example, if your network is 172.31.0.0, add the line **255.255.0.0 172.31.0.0**. (*Note*: You can add lines for any networks that should be able to access the NIS server databases.) Save and close the file.

7. Open the /etc/ypserv.conf file in a text editor. Uncomment the last line so that all hosts are allowed to access all databases. Save and close the file.

8. At the command prompt, type **service ypserv start** and press **Enter**. If you were setting up NIS permanently, you would also enter the chkconfig ypserv on command to add this service to the list of services that start when Linux boots. Because you're setting up NIS only as an example, don't enter this command.

9. Type **service yppasswdd start** and press **Enter**. (Again, if you were setting up NIS permanently, you would use the chkconfig command to start yppasswdd when the system starts.)

10. To create the NIS databases, type **/usr/lib/yp/ypinit -m** and press **Enter**. At the first prompt, press **Ctr+D** and then press **Enter**. At the prompt Is this correct? [y/N], press **Enter**.

11. Type **service ypbind start** and press **Enter**. Your NIS server is ready to go. (Because you need a client to test the server, you're skipping this step in this lab.)

12. Restart your computer if you're continuing to the next lab; otherwise, shut down the computer.

13

Review Questions

1. What's the purpose of NIS?

   a. Sets up a network file system

   b. Allows sharing all files between Linux computers

   c. Creates a Windows-compatible domain

   d. Synchronizes files, such as `passwd` and `hosts`

2. Which command causes the `ypserv` service to start when the system starts?

   a. `init ypserv yes`

   b. `chkconfig ypserv on`

   c. `config ypserv enable`

   d. `service ypserv boot`

3. Which file determines the network that NIS clients can connect from?

   a. `ypserv.conf`

   b. `makefile`

   c. `securenets`

   d. `network`

4. The NIS server package is installed, but it must be configured before you can use it. True or False?

5. Part of NIS configuration is specifying a domain name. True or False?

Lab 13.3 Working with the Firewall

Objectives

In this lab, you work with the firewall in the Linux GUI and learn how to allow and prevent services from accessing your computer.

Materials Required

This lab requires the following:

- A computer running Fedora 13 Linux
- A network connection and the IP address of another device on your network

Estimated completion time: 10 minutes

Activity

1. Start Linux and log in to the GUI as a regular user. Open a terminal window, and then type **ifconfig** and press **Enter** to view your IP address. Make a note of it, and then close the terminal window.

2. Click **System**, point to **Administration**, and click **Firewall**. Type the root password when prompted, and then click **Authenticate**. To view and change firewall settings, you need root privileges.

3. Scroll through the Trusted Services pane of the Firewall Configuration dialog box and examine the available services. Clicking a check box next to a service allows it through the firewall. Notice that SSH is allowed because it's a secure protocol.

4. Click **Other Ports** on the left. You should see the Telnet service listed because you added it in Lab 13.1. Click **telnet** and then **Remove** to prevent Telnet from accessing the computer.

5. Click **ICMP Filter** on the left. ICMP messages include messages sent and received by ping as well as status and control messages. By default, all ICMP messages are allowed to pass through the firewall. If you want to disallow certain ICMP messages, you click the check boxes next to them (see Figure 13-2).

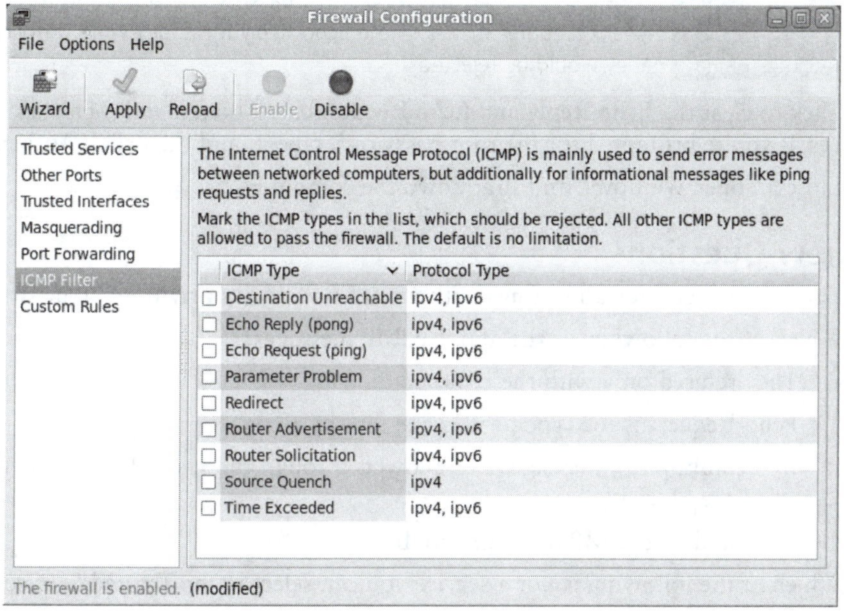

Figure 13-2 Configuring an ICMP filter

Source: Fedora Linux (*http://fedoraproject.org*)

6. To verify that you can ping your computer from another computer, go to another Windows or Linux computer, and at a command prompt, type **ping** *ip-address* and press **Enter** (replacing *ip-address* with the IP address of your Linux computer). You should see the ping replies.

7. On your Linux computer, click the **Echo Request** check box, click **Apply**, and then click **Yes**. If you're prompted for the root password, type it, and then click **Authenticate** to specify rejecting incoming ping messages.

13

The message sent by the `ping` command is called an Echo Request, and the message the target computer returns is called an Echo Reply.

8. Try the same `ping` command you used in Step 6. The `ping` messages time out.

9. On the Linux computer, click the **Echo Reply** check box, click **Apply,** and then click **Yes.** If you're prompted for the root password, type it, and then click **Authenticate** to specify that the firewall reject Echo Reply messages.

10. On your Linux computer, open a terminal window. Type **ping** *ip-address* and press **Enter** (replacing *ip-address* with the IP address of another device on your network). After seeing that that the `ping` messages are successful, press **Ctrl+C** to stop the `ping` command.

Even though you've told your computer to reject Echo Reply messages, the firewall always accepts packets in response to a request your computer makes. If the Echo Reply messages were unsolicited, they would be rejected.

11. Click to clear the **Echo Reply** and **Echo Request** check boxes, and then click **Apply.** Click **Yes.** If you're prompted for the root password, type it, and then click **Authenticate.**

12. Close all open windows, and shut down the computer.

Review Questions

1. You can change firewall settings with an ordinary user's privileges. True or False?

2. Which of the following is true about ICMP messages?

   a.   They're used only with the `ping` command.

   b.   Echo Request is the type of message sent by `ping`.

   c.   By default, `ping` messages are allowed through the firewall, but other ICMP messages are blocked.

   d.   By default, all ICMP messages are blocked.

3. Which of the following is *not* a service you can select in the Trusted Services pane of the Firewall Configuration dialog box?

   a.   FTP

   b.   DNS

   c.   Telnet

   d.   SSH

4. What protocol does `ping` use to send Echo Request messages?

TROUBLESHOOTING, PERFORMANCE, AND SECURITY

Labs included in this chapter

- Lab 14.1 Validating Files
- Lab 14.2 Using SSH
- Lab 14.3 Generating Public and Private Keys
- Lab 14.4 Exchanging and Signing Keys
- Lab 14.5 Encrypting Files

CompTIA Linux+ Exam Objectives

Objective		Lab
103.4	Use streams, pipes, and redirects	13.1, 13.4
110.3	Securing data with encryption	13.1–13.5

Lab 14.1 Validating Files

Objectives

This lab shows you how to validate files by using cryptographic hashes to verify that they're genuine. The md5sum command is one method for performing this task.

Materials Required

This lab requires the following:

- A computer running Fedora 13 Linux

Estimated completion time: 10 minutes

Activity Background

In Linux, you have a few ways to validate files, such as the sum, cksum, and md5sum commands. However, md5sum is cryptographically stronger than sum and cksum, so you should use it when possible. It uses the MD5 message digest to create a cryptographic hash of a file. When transmitting this file, you make the hash available to the recipient, who also uses md5sum to compute a hash on the file. If the recipient's hash is the same as the sender's hash, the file is genuine. If the hashes differ, the file has been tampered with.

A hash consists of 32 characters. Fortunately, you don't have to compare two long sequences of characters because md5sum handles this comparison for you if you use the -check or -c option.

Activity

1. Start your Linux computer. Switch to a command-line terminal (tty2) by pressing **Ctrl+Alt+F2**, and log in as any user.

2. To become familiar with the md5sum command, type **man md5sum** and press **Enter**. Read the information, but don't be concerned if you don't understand everything on the page. Press **q** to exit the man page.

3. To copy a program file in the bash directory to your home directory, type **cp /bin/bash ./** and press **Enter**.

4. To generate a cryptographic hash of the bash file and display the output onscreen, type **md5sum -b bash** and press **Enter**. The -b option is used on binary files, such as the bash program; by default, md5sum assumes the file is a text file unless you use this option. Output similar to the following is displayed:

   ```
   20b6100fa713bbd5591a74073fe622bca *bash
   ```

5. Generate the hash again, but this time send the output to a file by typing **md5sum -b bash > bash.md5** and pressing **Enter**.

6. To validate the bash file, type **md5sum -c bash.md5** and press **Enter**. You see bash: OK. The -c option is the same as -check, which tells md5sum to compare the MD5 hashes for the bash and bash.md5 files.

7. Next, you change the bash file by writing a few characters at the end of it. To do this, type **echo "123" >> bash** and press **Enter**.

8. Validate the `bash` file again by typing **md5sum -c bash.md5** and pressing **Enter**. Because the file has been modified since the hash was calculated, you see the following:

```
bash: FAILED
md5sum: WARNING: 1 of 1 computed checksum did NOT match
```

 The `md5sum` command uses the term "checksum" instead of the more precise term "hash."

9. Delete the `bash` file by typing **rm bash** and pressing **Enter**.

10. If you plan to continue to the next lab, stay logged in; otherwise, shut down your computer.

Review Questions

1. One disadvantage of using `md5sum` is that you must compare the long hash values yourself. True or False?

2. The `md5sum` command outputs its hash to `STDOUT` by default. True or False?

3. The `md5sum` command produces a cryptographic hash consisting of how many characters?

   a. 16

   b. 32

   c. 64

   d. 128

4. Instead of "hash," `md5sum` uses which term?

   a. Parity

   b. Checksum

   c. Block check character

   d. CRC

5. The `md5sum` command can check only binary files to see whether they're genuine. True or False?

Lab 14.2 Using SSH

Objectives

In this lab, you use Secure Shell (SSH) to communicate with another Linux computer.

Materials Required

This lab requires the following:

- Two computers running Fedora 13 Linux with a network connection between them

Estimated completion time: 20 minutes

14

Activity Background

In the accompanying textbook, you practice configuring and using Telnet. However, this protocol poses major security risks if it's used over a public network. It produces an unencrypted packet stream that can be intercepted easily. SSH is a more secure way to communicate because the packet stream is encrypted with a cryptographically strong cipher.

Activity

1. On one computer (called Computer1), switch to the second virtual console (`tty2`) and log in as any user. The other computer (called Computer2) must be running the `sshd` daemon. Fedora 13 normally starts `sshd` when the system starts, but verify that it's running by switching to `tty2` on Computer2, typing **ps aux | grep sshd**, and pressing **Enter**. If you don't see output indicating that `sshd` is running, ask your instructor how to start it.

2. To find Computer2's IP address, type **ifconfig** and press **Enter**. Make a note of this IP address.

3. On Computer1, connect to Computer2 via SSH by typing **ssh** *username@ip_address* and pressing **Enter** (replacing *username* with your login account name and *ip_address* with Computer2's IP address). You see output similar to this:

```
The authenticity of host '192.168.1.12' can't be established.
RSA key fingerprint is 3d:c1:c4:b4:24:df:f2:ef:ca:8f:f2:
62:34:51:5a:0b.
Are you sure you want to continue connecting (yes/no)?
```

In subsequent steps, remember to replace *username* and *ip_address* with your information.

The RSA key fingerprint is a 128-bit number expressed as 32 hexadecimal digits.

4. Type **yes** and press **Enter**. You see this warning:

```
Warning: Permanently added '192.168.1.12' (RSA) to the list of
known hosts. Mike@192.168.1.12's password:
```

5. Type the password and press **Enter**. The account's last login time is displayed followed by a prompt.

6. Disconnect from Computer2 by typing **exit** and pressing **Enter**. The following is displayed:

```
logout
Connection to 192.168.1.12 closed.
```

7. In Step 4, confirming that you wanted to continue connecting meant you trusted the other computer (the host) to be genuine. The host's key was then placed in your `known_hosts` file, which is stored in the `.ssh` subdirectory of your home directory. On Computer1, type **cd .ssh** and press **Enter**, and then type **ls -l** and press **Enter**. You see output similar to the following:

```
-rw-r--r-- 1 kenny users 682 2013-09-29 13:07 known_hosts
```

8. Use the `cat` command to examine the contents of the `known_hosts` file. You see output similar to the following:

```
192.168.1.12, ssh-rsa
AAAAB3NzaC1yc2EAAAABIwAAAIEA8qHgdWqbvt3c82WljCbOcF18tkxw
...
```

The first field is the IP address, and the second field is the host key. (If you had used a hostname instead of an IP address when connecting, the first field would be the hostname, and the second field would be the IP address.)

9. To see how SSH prevents connecting to a computer that's masquerading as legitimate, use a text editor to change one character (about midway through the key) in the `known_hosts` file so that the host key is different. Save and close the file.

10. Try to connect to Computer2 by typing **ssh** *username@ip_address* and pressing **Enter**. You see the following warning:

```
@@@@@@@@@@@@@@@@@@@@@@@@@@@@@@@@@@@@@@@@
@ WARNING: REMOTE HOST IDENTIFICATION HAS CHANGED! @
@@@@@@@@@@@@@@@@@@@@@@@@@@@@@@@@@@@@@@@@
IT IS POSSIBLE THAT SOMEONE IS DOING SOMETHING NASTY!
Someone could be eavesdropping on you right now
(man-in-the-middle attack)!
It is also possible that the RSA host key has just been changed.
...
Host key verification failed.
```

11. A host key might change when an administrator regenerates keys. When this occurs, you need to update the key in your `known_hosts` file. The easiest method is deleting that host's key in the file. Then connect to the host as you did in Steps 3 and 4. In this case, because there's only one key in the file, you can delete it, and it's re-created the next time you try to connect. To do this, type **rm known_hosts** and press **Enter**. Now connect via SSH as you did in Steps 3 and 4. After connecting, type **exit** and press **Enter** to close the SSH connection. Type **ls -l** and press **Enter** to verify that a new `known_hosts` file was created.

12. If numerous users on your computer connect to other computers with SSH, you can maintain a single `known_hosts` file instead of each user maintaining one. This shared file, `ssh_known_hosts`, is stored in the `/etc/ssh` directory. Switch to the root user by typing **su**, pressing **Enter**, and then entering the root password. Type **cp known_hosts /etc/ssh_known_hosts** and press **Enter**. Type **exit** and press **Enter** to log out as root. Delete the `known_hosts` file by typing **rm known_hosts** and pressing **Enter**.

13. Connect to Computer2 via SSH by typing **ssh** *username@ip_address* and pressing **Enter**. Enter your password to connect by using the `/etc/ssh/ssh_known_hosts` file.

14. Type **exit** and press **Enter** to close the SSH connection.

15. If you plan to continue to the next lab, log out but leave the computer running; otherwise, shut down your computer.

14

Review Questions

1. Before you can establish an SSH connection, you must run the `ssh` daemon on the client computer. True or False?

2. What's the size of the RSA fingerprint?

    a. 32 bits

    b. 64 bits

    c. 128 bits

    d. 256 bits

3. Where is the `known_hosts` file stored?

    a. `/etc/ssh`

    b. `~/ssh`

    c. `~/.ssh`

    d. `/var/ssh`

4. If a host key changes, what's the easiest way to place the new key in your `known_hosts` file?

    a. Copy and paste the value from a file.

    b. Type the information in the `known_hosts` file.

    c. Delete the key and re-create it by logging in again with SSH.

    d. Wait for the administrator to edit the `known_hosts` file.

5. A shared file containing host key information is `/etc/known_hosts_ssh`. True or False?

Lab 14.3 Generating Public and Private Keys

Objectives

This lab shows you how to generate public and private keys with the GNU Privacy Guard program (GPG).

Materials Required

This lab requires the following:

- A computer running Fedora 13 Linux

Estimated completion time: 30 minutes

Activity

1. Start your computer and switch to `tty2`, if necessary. Log in as root.

2. When an ordinary user issues the `gpg` command, error messages about memory not being secure are displayed. To suppress these messages and make gpg operation more secure, set the SUID bit by typing **chmod u+s /usr/bin/gpg** and pressing **Enter**.

3. Log out, and then log in as an ordinary user.

4. Generate public and private keys by typing **gpg --gen-key** and press **Enter**. You see this output:

```
gpg (GnuPG) 2.0.14; Copyright (C) 2009 Free Software
Foundation, Inc.
...
Please select what kind of key you want:
(1) RSA and RSA (default)
(2) DSA and Elgamal
(3) DSA (sign only)
(4) RSA (sign only)
Your selection?
```

5. To accept the default selection, RSA and RSA, press **Enter**. You see a message prompting you to set the key size. Note that RSA keys can be between 1024 and 4096 bits. Accept the default 2048-bit key size by pressing **Enter**. You see the following output:

```
Requested key size is 2048 bits
Please specify how long the key should be valid.
0 = key does not expire
<n> = key expires in n days
<n>w = key expires in n weeks
<n>m = key expires in n months
<n>y = key expires in n years
Key is valid for? (0)
```

6. Accept the default setting, 0, by pressing **Enter**. A message stating that the key doesn't expire is displayed, and then you're prompted to confirm this setting. Press y and then **Enter** to confirm that you want a perpetual key.

7. To construct a user ID for identifying your key, type your full name and press **Enter**. When prompted, type your e-mail address and press **Enter**. When prompted to enter a comment, type some text describing you, your family, or your company and press **Enter**. This comment is visible to anyone who has your public key. You see output similar to the following:

```
You selected this USER-ID:
"Mike Williams (Comment information) <mw@example.com >"
Change (N)ame, (c)omment, (E)mail or (O)kay/(Q)uit?
```

8. You can change any of the information you entered in Step 7. When you're finished, press O and then **Enter**. When prompted to enter a passphrase, type one and press **Enter**. The most secure passphrases consist of combinations of numbers, lowercase and uppercase letters, and symbols.

9. When prompted, enter the passphrase again and press **Enter**. You see output similar to the following:

```
We need to generate a lot of random bytes. It is a good idea to
perform some other action (type on the keyboard, move the mouse,
utilize the disks) during the prime generation;
...
```

14

10. When you see a message verifying that you've created your key pair, take a look at the first few lines of output. You should see something similar to key 86B9D4C3. Make a note of this key specifier. A new directory, called .gnupg, is created as a subdirectory of your home directory. Switch to this subdirectory by typing **cd ~/.gnupg** and pressing **Enter**.

11. Type **ls -l** and press **Enter**. You see output similar to the following:

```
total 24
-rw   1 Mike Mike 8075 2013-09-28 17:46 gpg.conf
-rw   1 Mike Mike  932 2013-09-28 18:50 pubring.gpg
-rw   1 Mike Mike    0 2013-09-28 17:46 pubring.gpg~
-rw   1 Mike Mike  600 2013-09-28 18:50 random_seed
-rw   1 Mike Mike 1069 2013-09-28 18:50 secring.gpg
-rw   1 Mike Mike 1240 2013-09-28 18:50 trustdb.gpg
```

    The pubring.gpg file is your public key, and the secring.gpg file is your private (secret) key. They're binary files, so you can't view them.

12. In case you forget your passphrase or your private key is lost or compromised, you need to have a revocation certificate that you can publish to others. Generate this certificate by typing **gpg --output revoke.asc --gen-revoke *key*** and pressing **Enter** (replacing *key* with the key specifier you noted in Step 10). You see the following:

```
sec 1024D/86B8D4C4 2013-09-29 Mike Williams (Comment information)
<mw@example.com>
Create a revocation certificate for this key? (y/N)
```

13. Press **y** and then **Enter**. You see the following output:

```
Please select the reason for the revocation:
0 = No reason specified
1 = Key has been compromised
2 = Key is superseded
3 = Key is no longer used
Q = Cancel
(Probably you want to select 1 here) Your decision?
```

14. Type **1** and press **Enter**. When prompted to enter a description, type **Key has been lost or compromised** and press **Enter**. Press **Enter** a second time to add a blank line.

15. When asked to confirm the description, press **y** and press **Enter**. You see output similar to the following:

```
Please enter the passphrase to unlock the secret key for the
OpenPG certificate: "Mike Williams (Comment information)
<mw@example.com> 2048-bit RSA key, ID 86B9D4C4, created
2013-09-29
Passphrase:
```

16. Type the passphrase you used when you generated your key pair in Step 8.

17. Type **ls -l** and press **Enter**. A plaintext file called revoke.asc has been added to the .gnupg directory. To view it, type **cat revoke.asc** and press **Enter**. You see output similar to the following:

```
-----BEGIN PGP PUBLIC KEY BLOCK-----
Version: GnuPG v2.0.14 (GNU/Linux)
Comment: A revocation certificate should follow
```

```
iGoEIBECACoFAkFaS1QjHQJLZXkgaGFzIGJlZW4gbG9zdCBvciBjb2
1wcm9taXN1
ZC4ACgkQ19exuIa51MQYDwCeMn0GIQjP98N05nGEFJpXed7R2PQAnj
POfhTkBJLoN7+nD8tgqg8L17vQ=GaeGjP98N05nGEFJpXed7R2PQAnj
...
-----END PGP PUBLIC KEY BLOCK-----
```

18. Log out, and then log in as another ordinary user. Repeat Steps 4 through 17.

19. If you plan to continue to the next lab, stay logged in; otherwise, shut down your computer.

Review Questions

1. If you lose your key or think it has been compromised, what should you do?

   a. Generate a new key.

   b. Notify the Webmaster of the GPG Web site and generate a new key.

   c. Submit a revocation certificate (prepared in advance) to a key server and generate a new certificate.

   d. Generate a new key by using a different e-mail address.

2. What's the minimum key size you can generate with the gpg command?

   a. 512

   b. 768

   c. 1024

   d. 2048

3. What's the default key size generated with the gpg command?

   a. 512

   b. 768

   c. 1024

   d. 2048

4. By default, keys expire in one year. True or False?

5. The comment you enter when generating your key is visible only to you. True or False?

Lab 14.4 Exchanging and Signing Keys

Objectives

This lab shows you how to exchange keys with other users and sign their keys, thus creating a "web of trust," which is a decentralized method of establishing authenticity between users. (The centralized method is using a certification authority to establish authenticity.)

Materials Required

This lab requires the following:

- A computer running Fedora 13 Linux

Estimated completion time: 30 minutes

14

Activity

1. Switch to `tty2`, if necessary, and log in as one of the users you used in Lab 14.3. The names Mike and Camille are used as examples; substitute your own usernames in these steps.

2. Mike and Camille want to exchange encrypted data with each other. To do so, they must place each other's public keys on their key rings. First, Mike needs to export his public key to a file so that Camille can import it. Type **gpg -a --export** *KeySpecifier* **>~/***UsernameKey* and press **Enter** (replacing *KeySpecifier* with the one you determined in Step 10 of Lab 14.3 and *UsernameKey* with the name of the file holding your public key).

 A key ring is a virtual container that stores public keys for people you're establishing a web of trust with.

3. Using the `-a` option in Step 2's command exports the key in plaintext (ASCII) format so that it's readable. Type **cat ~/***UsernameKey* and press **Enter**. You should see output similar to the following:

```
------ BEGIN PGP PUBLIC KEY BLOCK ------
Version: GnuPG v2.0.14 (GNU/Linux)
mQGiBEFaFO8RBAD9j4kkJjNRAAcIlJymGRB1DUZfwFadZwvPV7yjx0
IXvLDYB5rwHkwlFJhaRYwXALHld6PJ6jOAzwkCBtPwCvkCKFl+FS6N
...
------ END PGP PUBLIC KEY BLOCK ------
```

4. Make sure Camille can read the file by typing **chmod 644 ~/Mikekey** and pressing **Enter**.

5. Log out as Mike, and then log in as Camille. Examine Camille's key ring by typing **gpg --list-keys** and pressing **Enter**. You see output similar to the following:

```
/home/Camille/.gnupg/pubring.gpg
------
pub 1024D/E6016194 2013-09-29
uid    Camille Williams (Comment
information) <cm@example.com>
sub 1024g/220814ED 2013-09-29
```

6. To export Camille's public key to a file so that Mike can import it, type **gpg -a --export** *KeySpecifier* **>~/***UsernameKey* and press **Enter** (replacing *KeySpecifier* with the one you determined in Step 10 of Lab 14.3 and *UsernameKey* with the name of the file holding your public key).

7. Make sure Mike can read the file by typing **chmod 644 ~/Camillekey** and pressing **Enter**.

8. To have Camille import Mike's key, type **gpg --import /home/Mike/***UsernameKey* and press **Enter**. You see output similar to the following:

```
gpg: key 86B9D4C4: public key "Mike Williams (Comment
information) <mw@example.com>" imported
gpg: Total number processed: 1
gpg: imported: 1
```

9. To verify that Camille's key ring now has Mike's key, type **gpg --list-keys** and press **Enter**. You see output similar to the following:

```
/home/Camille/.gnupg/pubring.gpg
------
pub 1024D/E6016194 2013-09-29
uid    Camille Williams (Comment
information) <cw@example.com>
sub 1024g/220814ED 2013-09-29
pub 1024D/86B9D4C4 2013-09-29
uid    Mike Williams (Comment
information) <mw@example.com>
sub 1024g/12B8E56D 2013-09-29
```

10. Log out as Camille, and then log in as Mike again. Import Camille's key by typing **gpg --import /home/Camille/*UsernameKey*** and pressing **Enter**.

11. To verify that Mike's key ring now has Camille's key, type **gpg --list-keys** and press **Enter**.

12. Because Mike is certain that Camille's key is genuine, have him sign it by typing **gpg --edit-key "Camille Williams"** and pressing **Enter**. You see output similar to the following:

```
gpg (GnuPG) 2.0.14; Copyright © 2012 Free Software
Foundation, Inc.
This program comes with ABSOLUTELY NO WARRANTY.
...
Pub 1024D/E6016194 created: 2013-09-29 expires: never trust:
-/Sub 1024g/220814ED created: 2013-09-29 expires: never (1).
Camille Williams (Comment information) <cw@example.com>
Command>
```

13. To sign Camille's key, type **sign** and press **Enter**. You see output similar to the following:

```
pub 1024D/E6016194 created: 2013-09-29 expires: never trust:
-/Primary key fingerprint: 63F9 F685 0C33 94EF 9DA2 0034 4885
159D E601 6194
Camille Williams (Comment information) <cw@example.com>
How carefully have you verified the key you are about to sign
actually belongs to the person named above? If you don't know
the answer, enter "0".
(0) I will not answer. (default)
(1) I have not checked at all.
(2) I have done casual checking.
(3) I have done very careful checking.
Your selection? (enter ? for more information):
```

14. You're assuming Mike knows that Camille's key is genuine, so type 3 and press **Enter**.

15. When prompted to confirm signing the key, type **y** and press **Enter**.

16. Type Mike's passphrase when prompted and press **Enter**. If you enter the correct passphrase, you see the Command> prompt. Type **q** and press **Enter**. When asked whether you want to save your changes, type **y** and press **Enter**. You're back at the shell command prompt.

17. Log out as Mike, and then log in as Camille again. Camille can now sign Mike's key by using Steps 12 through 16 as a guide.

18. If you plan to continue to the next lab, stay logged in; otherwise, shut down your computer.

14

Review Questions

1. Which command exports a key in ASCII format?

    a. `gpg -export -A`

    b. `gpg -a --export`

    c. `gpg -e -T`

    d. `gpg -t -e`

2. Which command displays a key ring?

    a. `gpg --list-keys`

    b. `lskeys`

    c. `gpg --show-key`

    d. `pkikey`

3. Users who want to exchange data by using public key encryption must have each other's private keys on their key rings. True or False?

4. When you use the `gpg --export` command, you're exporting private keys. True or False?

Lab 14.5 Encrypting Files

Objectives

This lab shows you how to encrypt files with public key encryption.

Materials Required

This lab requires the following:

  • A computer running Fedora 13 Linux

Estimated completion time: 15 minutes

Activity

1. Switch to `tty2`, if necessary. Log in as one of the users you used in Lab 14.4. The names Mike and Camille are used as examples; substitute your own usernames in these steps.

2. Create a plaintext file called `secret` in a text editor. Type **The sky is blue** to add some text that you want to share with Camille but nobody else. Save and close the file.

3. At the command prompt, encrypt the file by typing **gpg --recipient "Camille Williams" --encrypt secret** and pressing **Enter**. You've created an encrypted file called `secret.gpg` without destroying the original file called `secret`. Type **ls -l secret*** and press **Enter**. You see output similar to the following:

```
-rw-r--r--1 Mike users 17 2013-09-29 13:44 secret
-rw-r--r--1 Mike users 17 2013-09-29 13:44 secret
```

Normally, Mike would send the encrypted file to Camille via e-mail. Because Mike and Camille's home directories are on the same computer and Camille can read files in Mike's directory, you can skip this step.

4. Log out as Mike, and then log in as Camille. Decrypt the `secret.gpg` file by typing **gpg --decrypt /home/Mike/secret.gpg** and pressing **Enter**.

5. Enter Camille's passphrase for her key when prompted. You see output similar to the following:

```
gpg: encrypted with 2048-bit RSA- key, ID 12B8E56D,
created 2013-09-29
"Mike Williams (Comment information) <mw@example.com>" The sky
is blue.
You've successfully decrypted the file and displayed the file's
contents.
```

6. You want to send the contents to a file, so use the `--output` option by typing **gpg --decrypt /home/Mike/secret.gpg --output secret** and pressing **Enter**. You should have a file called `secret` in your current directory; its contents should be the decrypted file.

7. Shut down your computer.

Review Questions

1. When you encrypt a file to send to another user, you use your private key to encrypt it. True or False?

2. When you encrypt a file, gpg deletes the original (unencrypted) file automatically. True or False?

3. Which command encrypts the `financial` file?

   a. `gpg --encrypt financial`

   b. `gpgencrypt financial --recipient "Camille Williams"`

   c. `gpg --recipient "Camille Williams" --encrypt financial`

   d. `gpgencrypt financial`

4. Which command decrypts a file?

   a. `gpg --decrypt secret.gpg`

   b. `gpgdecrypt secret.gpg`

   c. `gpg --sender "Mike Williams" secret.gpg`

   d. `gpg --recipient "Camille Williams" secret.gpg`

5. When you decrypt a file, you can send its contents to a file with the `--file` option. True or False?

14